The San Damiano Crucifix
Which Spoke to Saint Francis

# Oracion De San Francisco

Señor, haz de mi un instrumental de paz.
Donde haya odio
Ponga yo amor,
Donde haya ofensa
Ponga yo perdón,
Donde haya discordia
Ponga yo unión,
Donde haya error
Ponga yo verdad,
Donde haya desesperación
Ponga yo esperanza,
Donde haya tiniebla
Ponga yo luz,
Donde haya tristeza
Ponga yo alegría.

Oh, Maestro, Que no busque yo tanto
Ser consolado, como consolar,
Ser comprendido, como comprender
Ser amado, como amar.

Porque,
Dando, se recibe
Olvidandose, se encuentra
Perdanando, se alcanza el perdón
Muriendo, se resucita a la vida eterna.
Asi sea.

# BLESSINGS BEYOND ONE'S WILDEST DREAMS

*COMMEMORATING*
*SISTER ELIZABETH OHMANN'S*
*SIXTY YEARS*
*AS A FRANCISCAN SISTER*

Ruth K. Meyer

# BLESSINGS BEYOND
# ONE'S WILDEST DREAMS

## *COMMEMORATING SISTER ELIZABETH OHMANN'S SIXTY YEARS AS A FRANCISCAN SISTER*

Compiled by Ruth K. Meyer
Cover photo of the Andes Mountains taken by John Kraemer
Copyright © 2011 Ruth K. Meyer and Elizabeth Ohmann, O.S.F.
ISBN-13: 978-1-934478-28-8
Year of publication 2011

Printed in the United States of America by

*This book is distributed by Roy and Ruth Meyer, Melrose, Minnesota, rmeyer@stcloudstate.edu, and Jackie and Charlene Ohmann, Greenwald Minnesota, jcohmann@meltel.net. All proceeds from the sale of this book will go to charity.*

# Contents

## Acknowledgments

Publishing Sr. Kizzie's stories has been an extraordinary experience. Although many people have contributed to this book, I take full responsibility for any historical or geographical errors and any interpretation errors in Sr. Kizzie's stories.

Thank you, family and friends, for sending stories and photos, and for editing, advising, and encouraging me. Special thanks to Roy Meyer, Micki Gilmer, Barry and Stacy Meyer, Harry and Mary Kraemer, John and Pat Kraemer, Lucy Wessel, Jackie and Charlene Ohmann, Janet Haas, Laura Haas, Sarah Haas, Mary Ohmann, Diana Peters, Terry and Sharon Kotsmith, Mary Gebeke, and Sue Goodman.

# Preface

These are Sister Kizzie's stories. **Blessings Beyond One's Wildest Dreams** commemorates her sixty years as a Franciscan Sister. From growing up in a small farm community in central Minnesota to ministering on the highlands of Peru and on the United States/Mexico border, Sister Elizabeth Ohmann – Sister Kizzie – has reached out to the less fortunate with dignity and grace. In the Spirit of St. Francis of Assisi, she has lived a simple life, working with her hands and with her heart. Through her example, she reminds us that we are all called to bring about justice and peace in our world.

After working with Sister Kizzie for a month in 2005 in Tucson, Arizona, I decided to compile her stories to share with family, friends, and the next generations. These stories are from her letters to family and friends, her seminar and conference presentations, the numerous articles she has written for a variety of publications, and from our many soul-searching conversations. Throughout this book, I have added commentaries in italics. These include my interpretations of events, historical and geographical notes, and my work and travel experiences.

Sister Kizzie's ten years as a missioner on the Altiplano in Peru was a lifelong dream come true. Peru, South America's third largest country, has three contrasting geographical regions: the western coastal plain, the rugged Andes in the center, and the eastern Amazon rainforest. It was in the Andes Mountains on the shores of Lake Titicaca at an elevation of 13,000 feet where the Franciscan Sisters opened a mission in 1962. A few years later Sister Kizzie went there to live and minister to the Aymara.

*To walk in Sister Kizzie's footsteps,* my husband, Roy, and I spent a month in 2009 traveling and working in Peru with Global Volunteers, a nonprofit organization based in St. Paul, Minnesota.

Along with twenty volunteers from all over the United States, we tutored boys and did odd jobs at *Ciudad de Los Niños*, an orphanage and boarding school for more than 300 boys located in Lima, Peru's capital and largest city. Global Volunteers organizes more than 200 service teams each year in more than a hundred locations worldwide. For more information on living, teaching, and working abroad, please visit their website at www.globalvolunteers.org.

Just as Sister Kizzie and my mother, Mabel Ohmann Kraemer, traveled in Peru during the 1970s, nearly forty years later my brother, John, Roy and I trekked the Inca Trail to Machu Picchu and boated across Lake Titicaca to visit the Uros. Life in the Andes Mountains has not changed much during that time.

After living at an altitude of 13,000 feet for nearly ten years, Sister Kizzie developed high altitude lung disease and returned to teach and minister in the United States. Her knowledge of Spanish and her compassion for those less fortunate led her to the United States/Mexico border where she spent the last 25 years.

Over the years, reading her letters and essays about the human costs of migration evoked feelings of helplessness and curiosity. Sister Kizzie wrote about the undocumented migrants in search of higher paying jobs to better the lives of their families and communities. They come to work despite the fact that they are often exploited, intimidated, and paid less than United States citizens. Crossing the searing Arizona desert, they risk exposure, having their money stolen, and being raped, kidnapped, and beaten by bandits and smugglers. They risk death by dehydration on what often is an eight-day walk across the desert.

I spent January of 2005 with Sister Kizzie in Tucson to see, experience, and to learn more about the crisis on our border. I worked with Humane Borders digitizing tapes of news events and documentaries. This was truly an education as I had the opportunity to view all tapes. While in Tucson, I visited inland

and border cities in Mexico and went into the desert to check water stations and pick up trash. I learned firsthand what Sister Kizzie meant when she wrote the following to the family.

> God can be found in each day, in each event, and in each activity. Driving in the desert to place water for the migrant means getting up early, driving over rough roads, being attacked by insects and huge ants, getting sunburned, finding the flags and tanks vandalized, and finding a body of a migrant who died of dehydration.
>
> Driving in the desert also means seeing the spring wild flowers in bloom, seeing the ocotillo red-orange blossoms against the blue sky, enjoying the camaraderie with the drivers and other volunteers, sharing our work with visitors, reporters, and photographers, and occasionally meeting a grateful migrant.

This book is not a chronicle of Sister Kizzie's sixty years as a Franciscan Sister. Part One is about living her dream – working in the foreign missions in Peru and Ecuador. Part Two has stories of Sister Kizzie's first fifteen years working on the United States/ Mexico border. Stories of her next ten years with Humane Borders are found in Part Three.

From the elementary schools in central Minnesota to the Altiplano of Peru, Sister Kizzie is a teacher at heart. Part Four is about her teaching experiences in the elementary schools of the St. Cloud Diocese, tutoring her grandniece who suffered a massive head injury, and teaching in Ndoleleji, Tanzania and Yarnell, Arizona. Part Five includes her reflections on many topics, including her childhood, being a sister and a missioner, and living in a global community.

I, Ruth "Suzie" Meyer, am Sister Kizzie's niece. I was one of fourteen children born to Jack and Mabel Ohmann Kraemer. My

*Roy and I with five grandchildren. Back row: Luke and Colton*
*Front row: Mia, Jake and Drake*

family includes my husband, Roy, daughter, Micki Gilmer, son and daughter-in-law, Barry and Stacy Meyer, and five grand-children: Luke and Jake Gilmer and Drake, Colton, and Mia Meyer. I received a Ph.D. in Decision Sciences from the University of Minnesota and spent 37 years in education – 25 years at St. Cloud State University where I taught business statistics, coauthored statistics textbooks, and served as an administrator. My interests in an active retirement include traveling and volunteering around the world.

In 2009, I wrote **A Glimpse into the Soul of Africa** commemorating Father Dan Ohmann's forty-five years as a missioner in Africa. Father Danny is my uncle and Sister Kizzie's brother. It is for friends, family, and especially the next generations, that I believe documenting the passion and work of Father Danny and Sister Kizzie is critically important.

# With Gratitude
Sister Elizabeth Ohmann

As I sit back and think about where I came from, where I have been, and what I have done, I am filled with gratitude for the many blessings and opportunities I have received. For sixty years, my Franciscan Community has wholeheartedly supported me. Their constant prayers have filled me with continual joy and the strength to open my heart to different people and cultures.

I am indebted to my family and friends who have supported me. The heritage passed on to me taught me what my ancestors did and what opportunities were left for me to do. I pray for the generations to come that you may learn from your heritage, and study and be open to the possibilities of where you might go and what you might do. You will find strength in yourself when you know the strengths of your heritage.

When I went to Peru and the United States/Mexico Border, I prayed, "God, there is someone here who needs help." God does not answer in words, but I think I knew what He would say: "Go to work. You can do it."

God does things through me that I do not understand. God does them in ways I do not understand. Let God do what God wants to do through me.

*Sister Kizzie celebrating sixty years as a Franciscan Sister*

## Who's Who of American Women

In 2007 Sister Kizzie was selected for inclusion in the 25th Silver Anniversary Edition of **Who's Who of American Women** as one of the leading achievers from around the country.

# Introduction

*Elizabeth Ohmann was the seventh of eight children born to John and Elizabeth Ohmann on March 9, 1933, in Greenwald, Minnesota. After a girl, five boys and a wait of five years, she was a most welcomed baby girl. Named after her mother – my grandmother, I have always known her as Kizzie. She says that at the age of two and a half, when her younger sister, Janet, was born, she could not understand how a mother could have more than one baby.*

*Kizzie attended grade school at St. Andrew's School in Greenwald and Sacred Heart School in Freeport. Following one year at Melrose High School, she finished her high school education at St. Francis in Little Falls, Minnesota.*

Living in small towns in rural Minnesota was like living in the country. With many Sunday afternoon walks along the railroad tracks, I developed an acute sense of observation and an appreciation of nature. With all the family members, I helped with our large vegetable garden. At times I accompanied Pa and my older brothers on hunting trips and became quite a sharp shooter. All these activities as well as growing up during World War II, experiencing blackouts, food and gas rationing with coupons, Pa building military bases, and my older brothers defending the country, were important preparations for my life.

*Kizzie was accepted into the novitiate of the Franciscan Sisters of Little Falls on July 31, 1951. She chose the name Sister Miriam.*

We received a new name on our Reception Day. That's the day we received the habit and officially became members of the

*Sister Miriam of the Franciscan Sisters*

Franciscan Sisters of Little Falls, Minnesota. I chose the name Miriam for two reasons. I liked Miriam of the Old Testament, the sister of Moses, for her part in leading the people. And I liked the feel of the name on the tongue and lips as it was pronounced.

*Sister Miriam made her life vows on August 12, 1956. Her desire to be a teacher led to a Bachelor of Arts degree from the College of St. Catherine with a major in elementary education and a minor in science. Kizzie taught in the elementary schools of the St. Cloud Diocese from 1954 to 1967.*

The years I spent teaching special-needs students were especially rewarding. I loved the children and shared their excitement in new discoveries and a newly-found love of learning.

*On May 1, 1967, Sister Miriam changed her name to Sister Elizabeth, a privilege granted to the religious by the Ecumenical Council. Friends and relatives were pleased because she could again be called by her childhood nickname, Sister Kizzie.*

During or right after Second Vatican Council, we were given the choice of retaining our new name or going back to our baptismal name. I chose to return to my baptismal name because I like the name Elizabeth. I had been named after my mother and I was proud of that. Also I had been known by Elizabeth longer than I had used the name Miriam. Elizabeth was my legal name, so I did not need any proof that Miriam and Elizabeth were one and the same person.

*In 1967, Sister Kizzie's dream of entering the missions became reality. She received her Mission Cross from the Most Reverend Peter Bartholome, Bishop of the Diocese of St. Cloud in central Minnesota. For the next ten years, she worked in the*

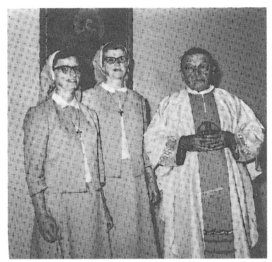

*Mission Crosses from Bishop Bartholome*

missions in Peru among the Aymara Indians along the shores of Lake Titicaca in the Andes Mountains.

The ways of the Lord are strange. From the day I learned to read, I was interested in the foreign missions and becoming a missioner. In the early 1960s, the Franciscan Sisters became involved in foreign missions and a few years later, my dream became a reality. I was going to Peru!

*After living at an altitude of 13,000 feet for nearly ten years, Sister Kizzie developed high altitude lung disease and had to move to a lower altitude. She came back to live in the United States in June of 1976.*

*Always a teacher at heart, Sister Kizzie returned to the classroom, and soon after, became a student. In 1983, she earned a Master's Degree in Christian Heritage from the Maryknoll School of Theology in Maryknoll, New York. This opened the doors to pastoral ministry and adult education.*

*Gifted with an organizing mind and strong leadership qualities, Sister Kizzie served as Administrator of the Motherhouse in Little Falls from 1983 to 1985. She has always been deeply concerned for the sisters, particularly the elderly who have retired to the Motherhouse. She encouraged the older sisters to help in any way possible and to pass on their wisdom to the younger sisters.*

*Sister Kizzie thought of the older sisters as a powerhouse of prayer and called upon them regularly, especially when she moved to Arizona in 1985. Her knowledge of Spanish led her to the dioceses of Phoenix and Tucson which welcomed Spanish-speaking sisters. She taught English as a Second Language, developed and taught a curriculum in Spanish to English-speaking students in the Catholic Schools, assisted Spanish-speaking families in religious education, and did pastoral ministry in parishes with large Hispanic populations.*

My greatest life-changing experiences have been to live with and become a part of other cultures, and to learn that there are many ways to live, to do something, and to be. Ours isn't necessarily the correct way, nor the best. Being able to move into and adapt to various cultures have indeed been blessings. Another blessing is the privilege of encountering and working with many religions. The similarities and faith we share have become so important that the differences are not the focus.

*For two years Sister Kizzie coordinated retreats at Picture Rocks Retreat Center. Then the opportunity to conduct study seminars to Mexico with BorderLinks presented itself. At that time, much of the activity along the United States/Mexico border was centered on migrants who came across the border, many illegally, looking for work. They were mainly interested in earning some money to feed their families or to improve their living conditions.*

*In 2000 Sister Kizzie gathered with a group to reflect on the increasing number of migrant deaths in the desert. It was the beginning of Humane Borders and Sister's next challenge. Based on a faith perspective, the organization's goals are to save lives by offering water to those crossing the desert and to advocate for changes in immigration policy.*

We are living in an important and exciting time in history. The world is becoming a world community and the church is becoming a church community. It is our privilege to help in this process of evolution.

*Sister Kizzie finds the coming together of peoples of many cultures and languages to be stimulating and provocative. There are more similarities than there are differences. In the Spirit of St. Francis, Sister finds the good in all people and events.*

Sixty years of living the Franciscan life has been a time of many changes. From being educated and teaching during the pre-Vatican II days to moving through changes into a new era. From growing up in the farmlands of central Minnesota to continuing growth in the highlands of Peru. From a Catholic community to an ecumenical community. From national churches to a global church. From a single-cultural surrounding to a multi-cultural surrounding. From a two-language environment to a four-language environment.

These and many other enriching experiences have opened my mind and my heart and soul – ***beyond even those where my wildest dreams have taken me.*** I am truly grateful for the opportunities and for the graces which have given me the courage to go where I feared to go, and to learn what I dared not to learn. As I look back, and at the same time glimpse forward, I find life is a blessing as big as the universe and beyond.

*In November 2010, Sister Kizzie was named Volunteer of the Decade for her work with Humane Borders. The following tribute was written by Sue Goodman of Humane Borders.*

## Volunteer of the Decade, 2000 to 2010
Sue Goodman

In Luke 8 we hear the parable of the sower who went out to sow seed. One seed fell on good ground. It came up and yielded a crop, a hundred times more than was sown. Like the sower, Sister Elizabeth Ohmann planted a seed on good ground. It sprang up and became Humane Borders, a humanitarian aid organization in southern Arizona that grew rapidly and received worldwide attention for the simple act of giving water to thirsty people.

It has often been said that Sister Elizabeth was with Humane

*The plaque Sister Kizzie received from Humane Borders, November 2010*

7

Borders before there was a Humane Borders. She is one of three people who had the idea to do something about migrant deaths in the spring of 2000, a year when 44 migrant deaths in the desert were recorded, most from dehydration. Little did anyone know that ten years later migrants by the hundreds would still be dying in the desert.

Sister Elizabeth holds a unique place of distinction among the estimated 15,000 Humane Borders' volunteers as the only person providing continuously active volunteer service since the moment of conception of her idea to address migrant deaths in southern Arizona. Her strong personal commitment and Christian compassion serve as a shining example for others to emulate.

In Matthew 25 Jesus said, "What you do for the least of these, you do for me." What has Sister Elizabeth done for the least of these? She has worn many hats while saving lives and nurturing the growth and development of Humane Borders, an organization which has grown to encompass the building of relationships with a wide variety of entities and individuals. Sister Elizabeth's participation in the formation and maintenance of these relationships has been and continues to be instrumental in the success of the organization.

When asked if there were any fears about carrying out the mission, she replied, "To find people who are very, very ill, and need medical help which we cannot provide – and fear that they cannot get to the hospital on time. Based on what I've heard, dying of dehydration is a very painful way to die."

When asked why she was motivated to get involved, she replied, "The people were suffering in the desert. I suppose the fact that I am a Christian and a Franciscan, I consider everyone my brother and sister. I have a hard time seeing any of my brothers or sisters suffer in the desert. I consider the desert to be hot, dry, and deadly."

On behalf of more than 15,000 volunteers, countless migrants,

Humane Borders hereby bestows the highest honor, respect and eternal gratitude for Sister Elizabeth's dedicated and extraordinary contribution of support for the mission to save lives. Like the sower whose seed yielded 100 times more than was sown, Sister Elizabeth's seed yielded more than a hundred water stations.

It is with joyful hearts that Humane Borders hereby proclaims:

**Sister Elizabeth Ohmann**
**Volunteer of the Decade, 2000 – 2010**
**Awarded November 13, 2010**

For I was hungry, and you fed me.
I was thirsty, and you gave me a drink.
I was a stranger, and you welcomed me.  Matthew 25:35

*Sister Kizzie at Humane Borders*

*Peru and Ecuador – Sister Kizzie's home in South America*

# Part One
# Missioner in South America

*The Aymara decided that we must love them very much,*
*more than anyone else did,*
*because we always had time for them.*
*This was the greatest compliment we have ever received,*
*or we ever could have received.*
                              Sister Kizzie, 1969


*In response to the Holy Father's call for greater involvement*
*of the Catholic Church in South America, the Franciscan Sisters*
*of Little Falls, Minnesota opened a mission in the Andes*
*Mountains on the shores of Lake Titicaca in 1962. The sisters*
*lived on the Altiplano doing catechetical and nursing work with*
*the Aymara Indians until 1979.*

*How did the nuns from Central Minnesota fit in with the*
*Aymara? Sister Kizzie wrote about their new life in Peru while*
*studying at the Maryknoll School of Theology in Maryknoll, New*
*York in 1982.*


The Franciscan Sisters left their homes, their environment, and their way of life to embrace the life of another. Their adaptation to a completely new way of life brought to the Aymara a sense of their own dignity. Their own simplicity of life led the sisters to be among the first to sit on the ground and share the food of the natives as well as to sleep on the dirt floors in the adobe huts. They didn't expect the people to treat them differently. The Aymara soon became aware that the sisters loved nature – their lake and mountains, their fields, and their humor. This reflected St. Francis' respect for all of creation. But mostly

*Sister Kizzie with Sister Rita Barthel*

it was the time that the sisters had for the Aymara that they appreciated. The sisters could be called on at any time, day or night.

*In August 1967, Sister Kizzie received her Mission Cross from Bishop Peter Bartholome of the Diocese of St. Cloud. She left her students at St. Mary's School in Alexandria, Minnesota to study Spanish for four months in Ponce, Puerto Rico. With money raised during Lent, the students from St. Mary's contributed $16 toward the purchase of Sister Kizzie's ticket to Puerto Rico. Although they were not eager to see her leave, her students wished her well in her future work in the missions.*

*The training course in Puerto Rico included Spanish, Latin American culture, anthropology, and history. Between classes, Sister Kizzie visited Fort Allen Naval Base and the St. Benedictine Monastery at Humacoa. She*

*Wearing the hat from her mission survival kit*

*Classmates at Language School*

*Having Mass on the mountain top*

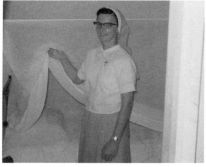

*Mosquito net – a necessity*

*Behind bars – a necessity?*

loved hiking in the mountains. Her favorite time was Mass on the top of the mountain with Fathers Tom, William, and Gerald. And Sister Kizzie loved swimming in the ocean. For someone who has always been afraid of water, she said swimming in the ocean was fun. "The gradual drop allowed us to walk out quite far. Then lying on the water, we rode the waves back to shore."

After studying in Puerto Rico for four months, Sister Kizzie was on her way to the Altiplano and a new life. Part One begins with stories of Sister Kizzie's ten years in Yunguyo, Peru living in the Andes Mountains among the Aymara Indians. This part also includes her work in 1999 in Ecuador where she was invited to spend a month with Sister Ramona Johnson.

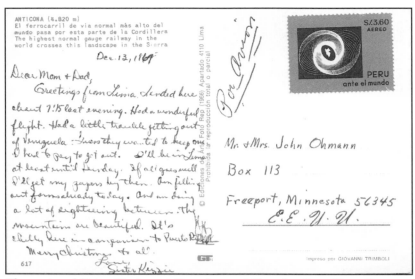

ANTICONA (4.820 m)
El ferrocarril de via normal más alto del
mundo pasa por esta parte de la Cordillera
The highest normal gauge railway in the
world crosses this landscape in the Sierra

Dec. 13, 1969

Dear Mom + Dad,

Greetings from Lima. Landed here
about 7:15 last evening. Had a wonderful
flight. Had a little trouble getting out
of Venezuela – there they wanted to keep one
I had to pay to get out. I'll be in Lima
at least until Sunday. If all goes well
I'll get my papers by then. Am filling
out forms already today. And am doing
a lot of sightseeing between . . the
mountains are beautiful. It's
chilly here in comparison to Puerto R___
Merry Christmas to all.

617                     Love,
                    Sister Kizzie

Mr. +Mrs. John Ohmann

Box 113

Freeport, Minnesota 56345
E.E. U.U.

S/.3.60
AEREO

PERU
ante el mundo

Impreso por GIOVANNI TRIMBOLI

*The postcard Sister Kizzie sent Grandma and Grandpa from Lima, Peru*

## Living on the Altiplano

*Map of Peru from WorldTravels.com*

*The Aymara Indians live on the shores of Lake Titicaca in southern Peru. Lake Titicaca, an inland sea formed by a volcano crater, is situated 13,000 feet above sea level. Nearly 140 miles long and 70 miles wide, the lake is almost evenly divided between Peru and Bolivia. From Lake Titicaca one can see the*

14

agricultural terraces with the snow-capped Andes Mountains in the distance.

The name Titicaca comes from the Aymara word meaning puma. A view from Gemini IX shows the shape of the lake as that of a puma chasing a rabbit. In a letter written to family, Sister Kizzie wondered how the ancients could see the shape of the lake.

*Map of Lake Titicaca taken from Wikipedia*

Did the ancients ever fly to get a bird's eye view of the lake to name it after a puma? At the mouth of the puma, which is ready to bite into the foot of the rabbit, is Yunguyo, my town, situated on a narrow strip of land.

There are about 5,000 people living in

*Lake Titicaca as seen from Gemini IX*

Yunguyo. Thirty-two communities surrounding the town form the huge parish of about 35,000 people. I went to Yunguyo and these communities to live and work with the Aymara Indians.

*Overlooking Lake Titicaca*

The Aymara Indians claim to be the only tribe unconquered by the Incas. They have clung to their own customs and their own language. The women dress in the traditional pollera (skirt), blouse, and derby. They carry everything on their backs, including their babies. This frees their hands to spin yarn as they walk. The men rarely carry the burdens on their backs. That is the job of the women. A donkey may be used to carry burdens if the family is wealthy enough to own one.

*White-washed adobe houses*

Their homes were mud huts built with adobe bricks made with mud, straw and water. In later years though, there was a sign of progress. Homes were constructed with bricks, covered with mud, and then whitewashed. Roofs were made of tin instead of thatch. Everyone in the family helped with the construction.

16

The Aymara Indians are a very family and community oriented people. At all of their functions, whether it was a community Mass, a wedding, a funeral, or whatever gathering, one of the main events was eating together. All the food (mainly potatoes, chuño, tunta, okra and beans – some from every family) was put on a blanket, creating a mountain of food.

*Sister blessing a boat on Lake Titicaca*

While this food was being mixed together, the men laid out the tablecloth, a piece of material 12 to 15 inches wide. The length depended on the number of people being served. The food was placed on the tablecloth and the people gathered. Women sat on the ground on one

*Dinner served on the long tablecloth*

side and the men on the other. After grace was said, all helped themselves to whatever food was before them. No food was ever wasted. Even a potato rolling off the tablecloth was wiped and eaten. After the meal, whatever food remained was taken home.

*Aymara ambulance*

*Sister Kizzie on her motorcycle*

For the Aymara walking was the usual mode of transportation. When that was impossible, for example, when an ambulance was required, a three-wheel bicycle was used. For longer journeys, the usual mode of travel was in the back of a truck. No matter how crowded, there was always room for one more. My motorcycle took me places where a car could not go.

Usually we went to the market one day a week. The market is like a department store without walls. One could purchase almost anything at the market. Brightly colored polleras (skirts) could be found in all colors and sizes. Vendors set out their wares, some on the ground, some on tables, and some in

*Always room for one more*

18

*Colorful polleras (skirts)*

*Sister Kizzie in the fruit department*

*Finding the ideal selling site*

*Tomas Tintaya making ice cream*

carts, always in the best-selling locations. They sold many things – from ice cream to drinks, candy, meat, zippers, bobby pins, even tablecloths. Ice cream was made when it hailed, or in the winter when the Aymara went to Lake Titicaca to collect ice.

Most of the trade was by barter. Payment for services was made in unusual ways. For example, they traded some eggs, cui

*Candy lady, Josepha, earns pennies*

*Going to the market*

*Christmas lamb named Navidad*

*Raising guinea pigs*

(guinea pig), chicken, sheep, or a hand-woven cloth. Once Sister Ramona was given a puma for delivering a baby. One Christmas gift was a lamb which we named Navidad.

*The Altiplano is often called the land of the llamas. Sister Kizzie wrote about her pet llamas, Rosita and Juancito.*

Living in the Peruvian Andes, I wanted a llama for a pet. Specifically I wanted a white baby llama. Within a short time, it became clear that it would be impossible to buy a baby llama. Mothers and babies were never separated. One of the campesinos (farmers) suggested that I look for a pregnant llama. He knew that another farmer had one, so within minutes we were visiting with him. The farmer thought it was a very strange request, but agreed he

*Sister Kizzie with Rosita and Juancito*

would sell the pregnant llama named Rosita for 600 pesos. I agreed, but asked how I could be sure that Rosita was pregnant. He said, "You just look at her, and you know."

Well, I could not see that Rosita was pregnant, so we wrote out an agreement. If the baby never arrived, I could bring the llama back and my money would be returned.

Then I asked when we should expect this baby. "Would it be my Christmas present?"

The farmer was sure that I would have a Christmas baby. Christmas came and went. No baby. I went back to the farmer who told me, "Don't worry. You need to have patience with llamas. Wait a few more weeks."

The first half of January came, and went. No baby. Again the farmer said, "Have patience."

February arrived. No baby. "Have patience."

Finally, the fifteenth of February was the big day. Rosita gave birth while I was at work. When I went home for lunch, the sisters gave me the news. I really wanted to pet this baby, but

21

how does one catch a baby llama who has just found its legs and was eager to use them? Sister Grace Skwira came to the rescue. She had grown up on a farm and knew how to catch calves. Sister Grace approached the baby llama from the side and quickly grabbed the baby around its neck.

The baby's hair was so soft and long that my whole hand would get lost in it. I named the baby Juancito, *Little John,* for my dad. The llamas stayed in the yard and became our lawn mowers.

*Before the baby llama was born, Sister Kizzie bought another llama named Antonio. He kept Rosita company.*

Rosita seemed so lonely in our yard. So I got a companion for her – Antonio. Rosita and Antonio got along very well together. After the baby was born, Antonio was no longer needed to keep Rosita company. I suggested we butcher him, and have a cookout for the missioners and all their workers and families. Butchering a pet, an animal with a name, was not acceptable. It took a lot of convincing, but finally we did it. I noticed that most of the people at the cookout did not eat the meat.

*A snow llama in a rare snow fall*

*Sister Kizzie's expertise with a gun is widely known among her family and friends. A favorite story is about her hunting trip in the Rift Valley in Africa when she camped with*

22

*her brother, Father Danny, and my parents, Jack and Mabel Kraemer, more than thirty years ago. Sister shot a gazelle. At that time, hunting was legal on the African plains.*

*Easier to shoot a pet duck than a wild duck*

Somehow it became known that my brothers taught me how to shoot, and occasionally I would hunt with my dad and brothers. One day I was invited by one of the priests to go hunting. At the least sound, the ducks living on Lake Titicaca would dive into the water. It was said that if a duck heard a shot, it would be under the water before the bullet reached it. I shot at a duck, hit it, and walked into the lake to retrieve it. As I walked out of the lake, a woman came running and screaming that I had shot her duck. We gave her the duck and money to buy another. She was satisfied, but not happy.

## Preparing Tunta and Chuño

The Aymara have used the method of freeze drying to preserve foods for many years, maybe centuries,

*Sister Kizzie pulling the first potato hill*

23

*Sister Kizzie at the potato guardhouse*

before it was adapted in the space age.

Tunta and chuño are freeze-dried potatoes. To prepare tunta, the potatoes are soaked in water for several weeks, either at the edge of the lake or in the ditches along the roads. Then they are laid out on the ground along with other fresh potatoes which would become chuño. The potatoes freeze during the night. The next day the bright sun thaws them. The Aymara then dance on these potatoes to squash out the moisture, turning them over with their toes so the sun can thaw the other side too.

This process of freezing and thawing goes on daily for two or three weeks until the process is completed. The guard located at a guardhouse watches the potatoes day and night. When ready, the tunta turns white as chalk and the chuño looks like little black rocks. Now these will never spoil. Tunta and chuño can be saved for winter, possibly forever.

*Checking the refrigerator*

*The Aymara mainly eat potatoes and other vegetables. On feast days or other special occasions, they may have the meat of guinea pigs, called cui, and the*

24

meat of other
animals hunted for
their feathers and
skins. *The seeds of
the native grain
called quinoa are
used as a staple.*

*Sister Kizzie
wrote the following
articles about
living with the
Aymara Indians for
the Franciscan
Sisters'* Echoes
From the Andes *in
1976.*

*Visiting while clothes are drying*

## God Provides

It doesn't take the Aymara long to help themselves when something is needed. With the faith they have, they believe that God will provide what they need and when they need it!

It isn't every day that one needs a ladder, so why should one have a ladder on hand all the time? When it is needed, it isn't hard to make. Just tie some boards across two poles.

## A Bridge is a Bridge

A bridge, according to Webster's dictionary, is a structure built across a river. The Aymara have never heard of Webster, but they know that at times it becomes necessary to get to the other side of the river. So they construct a bridge!

It may not be very solid, and it may have spaces big enough to fall through. But with careful stepping, it carries one across to the other side of the river. Who needs Webster?

*During her years in Peru, Sister Kizzie helped build several chapels. In 1972 my parents, Jack and Mabel Kraemer, financed a chapel in Accari, one of the villages close to Yunguyo. From negotiating the land to putting on the roof, Sister Kizzie managed*

*Sharing a beer after closing the deal*    *Breaking ground*

*Checking the chapel's arch*    *Ready for the roof*

*the construction. She went shopping with the men to buy materials. They would choose the materials, and she paid for them. Most of the manual labor was volunteered. But when Sister offered to help, the others quit working.*

### Rocks Serve Dual Purpose

*The finished chapel in Accari*

Rock walls are used for boundaries as well as for walking upon, and subsequently can change from one to the other within minutes.

I visited one of the communities outside of Yunguyo where the people were building a new chapel. A beautiful spirit of cooperation and unity is shown among the Aymara at such a time. The day for work was set and announced by the authorities. Every family sent someone to help work. The men mixed mud to be used for mortar and did the actual building. Some women carried the adobe bricks from where they were drying and baking in the sun to the building site. And other women prepared the meal.

*Putting adobe bricks on the back of a woman*

Rocks were cleaned and used to make the new road leading to the chapel. The width of the jeep was measured to make sure the road would be wide enough. The people did not realize that a jeep or a car cannot turn as sharp a corner as a person does when walking. The corners had to be changed from right angles to curves. What appeared to be a big problem ended up to be no problem at all. All they needed to do was move the rock wall over a few feet. The women carried the rocks to the new site. The men piled them up again, and the new rock wall was made.

Was there any opposition? Well, a little from the owner of the property. He lost a few feet of land and that could mean a row of potatoes. But what could he do? The community had been in agreement to build the road. It was built and the matter settled.

## Adapting to a New Culture

*When called to work among people of different cultures, Sister Kizzie acquaints herself with their customs and tries to adapt to their way of living. Often their ways are very different.*

### What is an Abrazo?

An abrazo is an embrace, or it could be a hug. Generally in Latin America it is a greeting. The way it is done depends on the area. In Peru an abrazo is a greeting. It is a handshake, then a very loose hug while patting the other person on the back with three light pats, then another handshake.

In some parts of Mexico it is a hug while touching right cheeks. In some areas it is touching, first right cheeks, then left cheeks. In some areas it is kissing the cheek.

This sounds very confusing and usually it is. I just watched and did what everyone else did. Otherwise I just put out my hand and sometimes just a handshake would do.

In Peru, one never left another person without a handshake. I tried that once while trying to end a conversation. I shook hands. The catechist had one more thing to say. When that was finished, or so I thought, I put out my hand again and we shook. But it wasn't ended yet. We shook hands six times before the conversation was finished.

I learned that it is not a good thing to try to cut off conversations.

### New Year's Day

Every year on New Year's Day, the teniente or mayor of each community is decorated in rings of bread, and paraded through the streets, walking or riding on a donkey. In the later years, the mayor sat on the back of a truck. The wife is also decorated with rings of bread, but she has to walk. The bread is not wasted. After the parade, the rings of bread are broken into pieces and shared with everyone.

*Teniente decorated with rings of bread*

### The Meaning of Time

One of my most life-changing events occurred in the early days of learning to live the culture and life of the Aymara people of the Altiplano.

On my way to the catechist meeting on a Thursday morning, I realized that I would be late. The meeting was scheduled for

9:00 a.m. My North American mentality told me to be there before 9:00. Since it was already 9:00 and I lived two blocks from the church, I ran – all up hill. Running uphill at an altitude of almost 13,000 feet is not a smart thing to do.

I arrived huffing and puffing and had to sit for five minutes to catch my breath. After my heart stopped pounding and my breathing slowed down, I could finally speak. I walked around and greeted the five or six catechists already there. Elisban, a catechist from the village of Sanquira, asked me why I ran up the hill.

"I was late and so I hurried." I responded.

He replied, "You ran, so you had to sit for five minutes before you could greet us. If you had walked, you would have arrived five minutes later and you could have greeted us immediately. The time would have been the same."

Without realizing it, the catechist was teaching me the most important lesson of my life. It was not the five minutes that were important, but the personal greeting of each catechist. After all, what is more important? The person or the minutes? The only really important thing is the NOW – being present at this very moment.

We began the meeting with only a few people. As each person arrived, that person greeted every other person before sitting down. The meeting was on hold for a few minutes.

Later I asked a few of the catechists to explain why that was done. After all, the latecomers had interrupted the meeting!

The catechists looked at me with sadness. "Don't you understand?"

I guess I didn't. So they carefully explained. "It would be very rude for someone to come into a room and just sit down without greeting everyone."

I explained that in our culture, we would be embarrassed if we came late and would try to sneak into the back seat without being noticed.

That would be very rude to the Aymara. To come in without greeting everyone was incomprehensible to them.

What a lesson! No meeting or Mass or gathering of any kind ever began on time. That gave us a wonderful opportunity to use that time to be with and talk to the people.

### Women Must Give Birth

Among the Aymara people, women do not have a place or value unless they give birth. They believed that if a woman did not give birth during her lifetime, she would give birth to a burro or donkey on her deathbed. The burro is the lowest of animals — only a beast of burden.

*Sister Kizzie with Godchild Julia*

I told them one day, "I am a woman and I don't have children. But I think that I am doing some good because I believe that I am doing what God wants me to do. I don't think that I will give birth to a burro when I die."

The people thought for a moment and said that maybe I was okay. I was white and I was a sister. But they added, "Si Dios quiere."

In English, they said, "If God wants." It is a common expression. Only if God wants, will it happen.

The Aymara were amazed that I was not interested in the color of their skin. I don't think God is either.

*Part One*

*After two years, Sister Kizzie realized that she needed to learn the Aymara language. She went to Cochabamba in Bolivia to study with a teacher named Miguel. Sister learned enough of the Aymara language to have some conversations with the people, but not enough to give homilies and talks. For these she had an interpreter.*

## More Than Repeating Words

*La Plaza in Cochabamba*

*Hiking Mount Tunari in Bolivia*

The Aymara language is very difficult to learn. It does not follow the English or the Spanish thought patterns. Though the grammar is not complicated, the pronunciation is almost impossible for English-speaking people.

During the first two weeks of language school, all I did was repeat sounds and words. The sounds are very guttural, as is German. I did not have a problem with sounds. I was simply a parrot repeating words but had no idea what I was saying. The teachers told me they had never before had a student from the United States who could imitate all the sounds. I guess no one else studying Aymara spoke German.

After learning a few words, I visited one of the islands in Lake Titicaca. I went to a house where I had previously visited, and greeted the lady in Aymara. She gave me an abrazo as though I were her long lost daughter. She chatted on and on and did not care that I understood very little of what she said. Her daughter in a wheelchair explained to me in Spanish how happy her mother was to be able to talk to me.

Little by little, one learns the language and customs of the people.

## Ministry to the Aymara

*Three missioners served the Assumption Mission in Yunguyo and the surrounding communities: Maryknollers Father Ed Arnold and Sister Julie McCarthy, and Sister Kizzie. They worked as a team in order to reach a large number of Aymara Indians in the expansive area.*

*Sister Kizzie wrote the following which appeared in* Echoes From the Andes, *a publication of the Missions of the Franciscan Sisters in November 1976.*

### The Kingdom ... is at Hand

"Go to the lost sheep, preach the message. The Kingdom of Heaven is at hand! Cure the sick, raise the dead, cleanse the lepers, cast out devils. Freely you have received, freely give. Do not keep gold ... for the laborer deserves his living."

The sending forth of missioners did not stop in apostolic times. Throughout the ages, missioners have been sent. Sister Julie McCarthy, M.M. and I felt this calling very strongly as we

33

*With Father Ed Arnold in the garden*

went out among the Aymara in the Altiplano of Peru.

"Go to the lost sheep." Christ said.

We listened and we went. The Aymara are a lost sheep. Centuries ago missioners came to them, baptizing them so they could be saved. All were baptized, and over the centuries this has been a priority among them. Up until now, all the newborn babies were baptized lest some evil befall them because of neglect.

But for many years the Aymara had no missioners, and no established local leadership in the Catholic Church. Natural leaders, their own catechists, arose and led the people. Their

*Warmer teaching outdoors than indoors*

Catholic religion had become a mixture of what the missioners taught and the beliefs of their forefathers.

The people were always happy when missioners came. They were more happy when the missioners came not only to visit, but to stay.

Their house became our house. They didn't worry if the house was clean, or if there was enough to eat, or enough blankets for the freezing cold nights sleeping on the mud floor.

Christ said, "Freely you have received, freely give." There was always room. The neighbors would learn soon of the visitors and extra blankets would arrive. When bread was scarce, they had potatoes. "The laborer deserves his living."

*With First Communicant Julia and parents*

*Sister Kizzie began by teaching religion to the First Communion class in the town of Yunguyo. She taught First Communicant Julia who was sick in bed and not expected to live. She was carried to the church to receive Jesus. Soon after, she started getting better.*

*Sister Kizzie taught religion in the Boys' School, the Girls' School and the Mixta. Students ranged in age from 9 to 22. After two years she believed she could reach more*

*Working with the catechists*

35

*Distributing the Body of Christ*

*students by assisting the teachers with lesson plans, audio-visual teaching aids, charts, and ideas. The teachers were most grateful, as religion was a required subject.*

*In addition the sisters taught the lay persons, the catechists, to be the leaders of the local church and to just be with the people – to visit their homes, their sick, their elderly, and their lonely.*

In the absence of a priest in the communities surrounding Yunguyo, the catechist was the lay leader in faith. I visited the communities when they had their weekly services. The catechist and I would plan the program for the liturgy; the catechist would conduct the service.

Together we discussed how the catechists could be better leaders and have more meaningful prayer liturgies of the Word of God. I also trained catechists to give baptismal instructions to parents and godparents, to baptize, to give pre-marriage instructions, to pray for the sick, and to bury the dead. Together,

*Fingerprinting before marriage*

the sisters and the catechists did the work of the deacon.

After marriage interviews and instructions, we took the couple's signatures or fingerprints. And I thought my hands were sunburned and weatherbeaten!

In the beginning, usually a sister would lead the worship services. However, before long, the catechist was leading the

*Tying the knot*

services and baptizing, while the sister again participated with the congregation.

In this way, she was doing what missioners hope to do – work themselves out of a job.

*Sister Kizzie wrote the following article about baptism for the Franciscan Sisters' publication Echoes From the Andes in November 1976.*

## Go, Therefore, and Baptize

Can the baptism of thirty cold, hungry, screaming babies be made a personal, meaningful, joyful experience in which new members are born into the faith and welcomed into the Church?

When there are so many people and they all come, one cannot say, "Go away. There are too many."

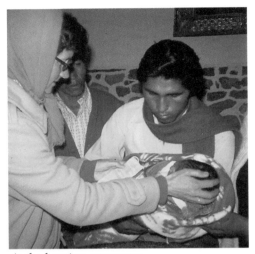

*At the baptism ceremony*

Then what is the answer? With a parish of 35,000 people and an average of thirty baptisms a week, one priest could handle each baptism individually, personally, and meaningfully – if that is all he had to do.

Is baptism the most important of priestly duties so that the majority of his time should be devoted to it? What will happen when that priest leaves and there is no replacement, as often happens? We, the parish team of Yunguyo, have considered these questions over a number of years.

The catechists who have representation on the parish team are the spiritual leaders in their own communities. They live among their people and know them and have time for them. A family with a new baby could go to the home of the catechist or to the community chapel and receive pre-baptism instruction from the catechist who was prepared to give it. The baptism ceremony could be performed in the community among the people with whom the child would live and grow.

At present there are five catechists prepared and approved to give instructions to parents and godparents and to perform the baptism ceremony. This is far from ideal as there are 32 communities and 35,000 parishioners within the parish limits of Yunguyo. But it is a beginning.

We are constantly working toward many ideals. For instance, we encourage parents to participate in baptism instruction before the baby is born. In this way the mother is also able to attend. A few Aymara were taking advantage of the opportunity. Again, it is a beginning.

Tomas Tintaya is among the chosen catechists who instruct and administer the sacrament of baptism. He does so for the parishioners of his own community as well as for his family. One of his first baptisms was his grandson Octavio.

*Father Danny with Tomas' daughters*

*In 1969, Sister Kizzie's brother, Father Danny, arrived from Tanzania, Africa where he is a missioner. He visited Yunguyo and several neighboring missions. He met Catechist Tomas Tintaya and his family, and blessed their new well. Together Sister Kizzie and Father Danny toured areas around Lake Titicaca.*

*Later Bishop George Speltz of the Diocese of St. Cloud in Minnesota visited his Peruvian friend, Bishop*

*Father Danny blessing a well*

39

*Bishop Speltz with Sisters Kizzie, Virginia Bieg, Colette Thoennis, and Adela Gross*

*Bishop Speltz with an Aymara family*

*Fedders. The bishops shared a mutual love for the Aymara children.*

## Teaching With Filmstrips

*One of the most popular programs of the year was a one-day mission in each parish community. A priest, another sister, and Sister Kizzie formed a team which they called a Campo Community because they worked in the campo or country.*

The Campo Community would spend a day with the people in their own community. The sisters would give instructions and hold discussions with the people while the priest would hear confessions. It was through these instructions and discussions that the team developed instructional filmstrips which were slides taped together to make a filmstrip.

The Campo Community took pictures of local people and local situations depicting the Gospel. The team wrote the script, paraphrasing the Gospel in real life situations. Initially they operated the adapted projector with bicycle power. Later they used a car battery for energy to run the projector.

At the end of the day, a family would invite the team to their home. They ate as the people ate, slept as the people slept, and became one with them.

*Sister Kizzie wrote the following which appeared in the 1977 Easter publication of* Echoes From the Andes. *Campesinos is the Spanish word for peasants or farmers.*

*Sister Kizzie with the bicycle projector*

**Instructions for Campesinos**

*A car battery to run the adapted projector*

Lent is a very busy time in our Yunguyo parish high in the Andes when everyone wants to go to confession. One morning Father Ed, Sister Julie, and I left in our jeep loaded with equipment. What a beautiful sight to drive up to

*Accompanying the hymns with the melodica*

a chapel and have anywhere from 100 to 400 people waiting to welcome us! After a brief explanation of the day's schedule, Father Ed began hearing confessions – sitting on a tombstone, or whatever was handy.

With the help of a catechist, Sister Julie and I showed a set of slides. These were pictures of their own people depicting the story of the Good Samaritan. One of our seminarians narrated the story in Aymara. During the instruction period, we discussed the practical application to our daily lives.

The response was heartwarming. Soon the people themselves were thinking of ways to imitate the Good Samaritan and become better Christians. During this year, more than ever before, the women responded – maybe because they realized that I could understand Aymara, although still in a very limited way.

A real feeling of community was shown as they prepared lunch for us. Every woman brought cold potatoes, beans, chuño, or okra, and placed them on one blanket, forming a mountain. A long narrow piece of cloth was laid on the ground. The men carried the lunch from the blanket and spread it along the cloth. The women seated themselves along both sides of the cloth at one end; the men sat or stood at the other end. Sometimes I joined the women, but usually I was given a special blanket to sit on. After grace was prayed, everyone reached for the food he or she desired. After lunch, if everything was not eaten, each woman gathered up a small portion to take home. No food was wasted.

Immediately after, preparations began for Mass. Depending

on the size of the community, Mass was in the chapel or outside. It seems we were outdoors more often than indoors. There was a feeling of community, as the people participated in the singing and Mass prayers, now in the Aymara language. The catechists or volunteers read parts of the Mass.

*With Sr. Theresa Karnowski and Padre Fidel*

The Aymara were grateful. No one left without giving us an abrazo of thanks. It was a long hard day. The body was tired but the spirit was happy.

## Quasimodo Sunday

*Walking in procession*

Quasimodo Sunday, the first Sunday after Easter, is also known as St. Thomas Sunday. On this day the sidewalks around the plaza are decorated with flower petals. Each community is assigned a section of the plaza to

*Receiving a flowered serpentinas*

decorate, sometimes in pictures, sometimes in symbols, and sometimes with the name of the community. After Mass, there is a procession with the priest carrying the Blessed Sacrament. It is very much like the Corpus Christi procession at home.

The priest carrying Jesus walks over the flower petals blessing them. Immediately after the petals are blessed, the people rush to pick them up to take home for tea or to feed the animals. Everyone knows that any person drinking the tea or any animal eating the petals would not suffer from stomach ailments during the year.

Woe to anyone who happens to be too close behind the priest!

*Sister Kizzie wrote the following story for <u>Echoes From the Andes</u> in March 1976.*

## Sharing Potatoes and More

"Which are the potatoes and which are the rocks?" Sometimes it seems a bit difficult to differentiate. However, Francisca, the wife of Catechist Tomas, doesn't seem to have any problem knowing which is which.

I had promised Tomas that I would be out to see him and discuss some of the problems he had concerning his work as a catechist in his village. I made the promise for a certain day and at a certain time. Since nothing is certain on the Altiplano, they weren't sure (and neither was I) when I would arrive until I did! Consequently no preparations were made for our meal.

*Drying cow dung to use for firewood*

After I arrived, Francisca and Tomas dug a hole in the ground and lined it with rocks. Using cow dung for fuel, they prepared a fire. After the cow dung had burned away and the rocks were hot, they threw potatoes into the hole, and then other rocks and dirt on top of the potatoes. While the potatoes baked for an hour or so, Tomas and I had time to discuss his work.

Francisca seemed to know the exact moment the potatoes would taste their best. She separated them from the ground and rocks, not missing any, and served them to us – steaming hot. Along with the potatoes Francisca prepared fasa. She dissolved a white rock in water like a thin plaster or like chalk in water. Dipping the potatoes in fasa added flavor.

Tomas and I enjoyed the baked potatoes without interrupting our discussion.

*Not very long ago while riding a bus in Arizona, Sister Kizzie was asked by a fellow passenger if she was ever afraid while she lived in Peru. She responded, "Never, except once, when I was accused of causing a hailstorm." Actually she was blamed for two hailstorms.*

## Hailstorms

Local customs and beliefs must be learned, or maybe experienced when adjusting to another culture. One of these experiences took me totally by surprise. I visited some sick people in one of the villages. I talked and prayed with each person while the padre and the family walked around blessing the house and property. Each family graciously thanked us for coming and wanted to give us gifts for doing so. We explained that we did not need any gifts. We were happy that we could visit them. That itself was a gift.

The following morning, rather early, Gregorio, the catechist from the village we had visited the day before, came to our door. He said to me, "Do not come to our village today as you had planned."

"Why?" I asked.

With a very strange look on his face, he responded, "The people will kill you."

I wondered why the people would want to kill me. I had visited them many times and the people always seemed happy when I would go to their village.

Gregorio explained. "This time is different. We had a hailstorm last night and the people say it is your fault that all the crops are destroyed. Whenever something bad happens, we have to find a reason for being punished by God. The only thing we could find was that you had walked out in the fields yesterday."

I thought for a moment, trying to figure out what to say. Finally I responded to Gregorio, "I will go out today because I had promised that I would come, and I do not want to break a promise. But before we go, I would like you to go to the church with me and ask the padre if he would go along as he also was there yesterday."

On the way to the church I wondered why it was my fault and

not the padre's. Gregorio explained that the padre had been there for years and they never had a hailstorm following his visit. But now the madre came along to visit, so it must be her fault.

The padre agreed that we must go back to visit. Thankfully the people decided that there must be another reason for a hailstorm or we would not have come back.

The second hailstorm I caused was more serious. This time there were three of us. The padre, Sister Julie and I were going together to a village. This particular village was quite far from town, so we often stayed over night. A family gave us a room. We threw our sleeping bags on the dirt floor for the night. In the morning Sister Julie and I went out to catch the water running from the roof to wash our faces.

There had been a hailstorm during the night. Rain water was running down the mountain carrying along anything that was in the way, leaving deep gullies. Part of one house very close to us was washed away. Half of the house was on solid ground; the other half had no foundation. I thought of the Scripture verse that reminds us to build on solid rock and not on sandy soil.

In a matter of minutes the local catechist came to tell us that the people were about to tip our car as we must have been the cause of the storm which caused their crops to be washed away. Sister Julie and I went down to where the car was parked. The padre was already there talking to the people. Sister Julie and I stayed by the car to protect it while all the people of the village and the surrounding area walked past to go to a meeting in the school. They would decide whose fault it was that they were punished by a hailstorm.

While we waited by the car, many people walked past us carrying walking sticks, which they never had done before. They didn't say a word of greeting. Among the Aymara it is the highest of insults to not greet someone when meeting.

At that moment I felt some fear and said to Sister Julie, "This is serious!"

We started greeting each person within earshot of us. Most of the Aymara didn't return the greeting. Suddenly a picture of a headline in the <u>St. Cloud Times</u> or the <u>Minneapolis Star Tribune</u> appeared in my mind, "Missioners in Peru killed because they caused a hailstorm."

At the school the padre asked if he could join the meeting. Julie and I stayed outside with the women. Women never could join the meetings. They waited outside. It seemed we waited a long time when the catechist, the padre, and some leaders of the village came to tell us that everyone agreed that we had caused the hailstorm and it was our fault that the crops were ruined. This time there were two madres and the damage was more widespread. I tried to explain that we had no power over the weather and we didn't think that God would use us to do harm when we came only to help them.

If it wasn't our fault, then whose fault was it? Someone said that a woman in the village had a miscarriage during the night. It must be her fault because the mother couldn't give life to the baby, but took a life instead. I asked the people to think of how much the mother was suffering, not only physically, but she just lost her baby. Let us not add more suffering to what she already has.

The men went back into the classroom for another session. Soon they came to the conclusion that if it wasn't our fault and not the mother's fault, then someone else must be at fault. Maybe someone had sinned and had not yet been forgiven. So if we agreed to go to the church with all the people and have a forgiveness service, and then we would walk through the fields and bless them so that their crops would be restored, we would be forgiven. No one would say it was our fault. We agreed.

The forgiveness service was one of the most touching and inspiring services that I have ever been a part of. Everyone in the village was there. The padre led the service with words of forgiveness from God, and forgiveness from one another. He gave absolution and then each person asked forgiveness of every person in the room. It took more than an hour for each person to ask forgiveness of one another. I even learned the words of forgiveness in Aymara that day.

Immediately we started walking through the fields. The padre blessed each one. By late afternoon we returned to the village only to find the catechist from a neighboring village waiting with a warning for us. "Don't drive past our village (the only way to go home), because the people will kill you."

We wanted to go home as we were tired and hungry. We wanted no more negations. Instead of walking and blessing the fields of the neighboring village in the evening, we agreed to come back the next day. Then we would have all day to walk and bless the fields. The catechist agreed and would tell his people.

They were waiting for us when we arrived the next morning. We spent another day walking and blessing fields. Blessing fields meant that we stopped at each field, said a prayer, and sprinkled the field with holy water.

### What Time is Mass?

Claudio, from one of the outlying communities invited us to say Mass at their chapel. When asked what time we should come, he pointed a finger up and tilted it a bit to the left. I asked what that meant. He said that straight up would be noon. A little to the left was shortly before noon or around 11:00 a.m.

It wouldn't make any difference. The right time was when the people actually came to Mass.

Eventually we learned that people would be there about an hour after they heard our jeep arrive. It took that long for those living the furthest distance to walk to the chapel. That hour was not lost time. It became the most precious hour of the day. We would meet and greet the people as they arrived, and find out who was sick in the community, who needed a visit in their home, who wanted their house blessed, or who just wanted to talk.

## Greatest Compliment

One of the greatest compliments that Sister Julie and I ever received came in the most unexpected way. We accompanied Father Ed to the community of Quimsa Cruz for Mass. After Mass I asked the catechists, Tomas and Gregorio, if they would ask the peoples' permission for us to leave immediately that day because I had another appointment in the village that afternoon. It was an appointment set quite some time ago which I really wanted to keep but was too embarrassed to explain why. I had set the time with a ham radio operator in the United States to make a phone call to my mother for her birthday. I even had to ask Mom to pay for the long distance call from the operator in the United States to her home.

The people of the communities we served knew that when Sister Julie and I visited, we always had the day to spend with them. Since we asked to leave right after Mass, we must have a very important reason. The people talked for ten, maybe fifteen minutes. Sister Julie and I wondered what they could be talking about for so long. It was all in the Aymara language so we did not understand them. We were getting worried.

Finally one of the catechists came up with the final word. It was decided that we could leave early because we never asked unless there was a good reason. The people decided that we must love them very much, more than anyone else did, as we always had time for them. This was the greatest compliment we ever have received, or we ever could have received. Again we learned that the only really important time is NOW – this very moment.

*Welcome to the Uros!*

## Traveling in Peru

One does not live in Peru, or visit Peru, without traveling around the beautiful country. Just as Sister Kizzie and my mother, Mabel, visited Lake Titicaca and Machu Picchu in the 1970s, my brother, John, Roy and I made the same trip in 2009. We boated across Lake

*Sister Kizzie with a Uros child*

*The depth of a floating island*

*Selling handmade colorful cloths*

Titicaca from Puno to visit the Uros on their reed islands. Later we trekked the Inca Trail to Machu Picchu.

Lake Titicaca is most famous for the population of people who live on the Uros. This is a group of about forty artificial islands made of totora reeds which grow abundantly along the shores of the lake. The islands are as large as city blocks and may have up to fifty people living on one island. The original purpose for building the floating islands with reeds was defensive, as they could be moved in case of a threat. Many reed watchtowers still remain on the islands.

Totora reeds are also used for the thatched homes and the picturesque boats. The Uros eat the roots of the totora reeds as a vegetable. We sampled the juicy and tasty root. The Uros fish, hunt a type of duck, and trade their colorful cloths along the shoreline of Lake Titicaca for other foods and supplies.

Walking on a reed island, we agreed with Sister Kizzie that

*A daughter watching her mother sew*   *Youngest person on the island*

*Beautiful, hand-crafted boats*   *Easy to row on calm water*

*this was a most amazing place to visit. We were not surprised to hear that the most serious illness the Uros acquire is rheumatism from living on totora reeds.*

## Machu Picchu

*Machu Picchu is the most spectacular archeological site on the eastern slopes of the Andes. Built by the Incas in the fifteenth century, the site is located 8,000 feet above sea level. Most archaeologists believe that Machu Picchu was built as an estate for the Inca emperor Pachacuti, but was abandoned when the empire collapsed under Spanish conquest.*

*Over the centuries the Inca site became surrounded by jungle,*

*Machu Picchu in the mountain forest*

*Llamas roaming freely*

*known only to local residents. In 1911, the American explorer, Hiram Bingham, rediscovered the lost city and brought it to the world's attention. Often referred to as the Lost City of Incas, it is the most familiar icon of the Inca World. Bingham and other historians believe that Machu Picchu is the traditional birthplace and spiritual center of the Inca people.*

*Machu Picchu is an amazing urban creation in the middle of a tropical mountain forest. It has 140 structures including temples, sanctuaries, and residences – houses with thatched roofs, huge walls, terraces, and ramps. There are more than one hundred flights of stone steps – some completely carved in a single block of granite. The Incas were masters at cutting and tightly fitting blocks of granite together without mortar. How they moved the enormous blocks of granite remains a mystery.*

*Preservation of the site is ongoing. Volunteers scrape the mold, lichen, and moss off the smooth surface of the granite. Llamas keep the grass tidy and are capable of reaching many spots inaccessible by lawnmowers.*

In 1981, Peru declared the area surrounding Machu Picchu a Historical Sanctuary. In addition to the ruins, the sanctuary includes a large portion of the adjoining region, rich with flora and fauna. In 2007, Machu Picchu was voted one of the New Seven Wonders of the World.

*Preserving the ancient city*

All visits to Machu Picchu leave from Cusco. Sister Kizzie and my mother, Mabel, took the 50-mile train ride from Cusco. John, Roy and I chose to hike the Inca Trail – a four-day journey from the Urubamba River valley up through the Andes Mountain range. Accompanied by guides, we slept in tents and trekked in the footsteps of the Incas on one of the world's oldest treks. We climbed more than 13,000 feet, passing

*Meeting on the Inca Trail*

*With John and Roy on a mountain pass*

glacial peaks and descending into lush green forests above the clouds. We passed several well-preserved Inca ruins and settlements before arriving at the Intipunku, the Sun Gate, on Machu Picchu Mountain.

## Leaving the Aymara

*After living at an altitude of 13,000 feet, Sister Kizzie developed Monje's Disease, a high altitude lung disease, and was forced to move to a lower altitude. She returned to the United States in June of 1976. A few years later, the other Franciscan Sisters left the Altiplano after serving the Aymara for seventeen years.*

## Living and Ministering in Ecuador

*During the month of July 1999, Sister Kizzie accepted the*

Map of Ecuador from worldtravels.com

*invitation from the Franciscan Sisters to volunteer in Ecuador with Sister Ramona Johnson. Ecuador, a country located on the Pacific Ocean in western South America, includes the Galápagos Islands in the Pacific. Its capital is Quito and its largest city is Guayaquil. Ecuador gets its name from its location on the equator.*

*The population of Ecuador is estimated to be nearly fifteen million people. Since Spanish is spoken as the first language by more than 90% of the population, Sister Kizzie quickly adapted to the language as well as the culture. In this part you will find stories of her daily life and ministry in Duran, a suburb across the river from Guayaquil. She lived and worked with 100,000 parishioners in the parish of Santa Marianita. This part also includes Sister's Kizzie's experiences during the country's difficult economic climate and strike, and her travels in Ecuador.*

### Living in Duran

The sisters lived simply in a house in which most of us probably would not want to spend the greater part of our lives. All the necessities were there, but little beyond. The sisters' house was built right next to the market and a very busy street. There was never a moment of quiet, day or night.

A mosquito found me the first day. He went home to inform all his relatives and friends that a new McDonald's had moved into the convent. It had soft skin to puncture, and sweet blood. They all came for a taste the next evening while I was in bed. I had been covered with a sheet up to my neck. In the morning I thought I had the measles. A bite under my left eye caused it to swell and turn black and blue. The other cheek was twice its normal size from so many mosquito bites.

*Sister Ramona welcoming Sister Kizzie*

Sister Ramona said I looked as though I had been in a fight. After that I taped the holes in the screens and sprayed my room. Once I learned how to control these little creatures, I was fine.

Otherwise, my health was good. Although toward the end of the month, I stayed close to home with a sinus infection and sore throat. I had too much ocean air and airy buses. After two days, I was up and around. While doing a little housework, I heard the fire emergency siren blowing. It was very loud as the fire station was directly across the street from the convent. I went to the window to watch. A fire truck was parked in the street; cars were driving around the truck. The siren blew again and the fire truck started moving slowly, but the cars kept right on passing it. After a short time I went back to work. About an hour later I heard a vehicle revving up the motor to keep it running, or so it seemed. Again I went to the window and saw a van move only a few inches after each revving up. It was an ambulance. It's not often that our street is quiet.

During the month I was there, our electricity was turned off twice but only for a few hours. I got ready for bed by candlelight, and after that I didn't care if there was light or not.

Water was a different story. That would be cut off for days at a time. When it came back on, we filled every available pail, a big kettle, and a big plastic container, which probably holds 25 gallons that we always had for emergencies. We took showers when the water was restored with the hope that it would last long enough to finish.

Even when there was water in the faucet, we couldn't drink it. We boiled it twenty minutes first. It was so different from drinking water directly out of the faucet as we do in the states. We often had to buy water – one kind for washing, cleaning, and flushing, and the purified water for drinking and cooking. We were extremely frugal with the use of any water. Yet this was better then what most people had in Duran.

One day toward the end of the month, the water was off again. We had clothes soaking in the washing machine. The next day we had no water all day. We used the water from the washing machine to wash dishes and to flush toilets. The electricity went off too, but only for about five or ten minutes. Usually that was a warning that soon it might go off for a longer time.

The third day there was still no water. In the early afternoon we got a call saying we'd have water for an hour. We filled every container. Always optimistic, Sister Ramona expected the water to be on longer than an hour. Both of us took showers. One must take advantage of the water when there is some. Shortly after that, the plumber came to fix the faucet in the bathroom. Again the water was turned off while he worked. Later in the evening, the faucet was fixed and we had water.

*Vendors and shoppers on the street*

Every day was market day, but Saturdays and Sundays were the big market days. Outdoor markets were all very much alike. They went on for blocks. You can find almost anything you need at the market.

Food is cheaper here than in the United States or Mexico. I went shopping one morning with 15,000 sucres – about $1.50. I bought

*Shopping in the meat market*

59

six bananas for 1,000 sucres, one papaya for 5,000 sucres, and a pound of grapes for 5,000 sucres. I came home with 4,000 sucres left. The total cost was $1.10. I expect that at some point the country will drop the three zeros so that 1,000 will be one sucre as Bolivia did when I lived in Peru.

One day a ten-minute trip to the market took me two hours. Right outside the market, a taxi hit a bicyclist. It was amazing how quickly people gathered in the street. Everyone was talking at the same time. Thankfully no one was hurt. Someone started directing traffic while the older men told everyone to leave. Soon all was as though nothing had happened.

A snack was served each time people gathered, whether it was Bible study, prayer meeting, or whatever. In the afternoon it might be a glass of coke and a small sandwich usually made with tuna spread. The crust was always cut off the bread. In the evening, it might be a roll and tea.

One evening, a child came to pick up the empty cups. She took mine, walked away, then turned and announced to us, "There is one drop left." She proceeded to drink it.

Birthdays were always special. We may have camarone (shrimp) sushi, fried corn, banana patties, and usually a coke. One

*Celebrating a birthday*

morning a woman's group celebrated a birthday. It was a time for them to forget everything else and enjoy each other. They sang and talked and laughed a lot – very loudly.

## Filling a Huge Need

*The sisters spent their time praying with the people, working with the Basic Christian Communities, visiting and bringing Communion to the sick and elderly, and tutoring children. Their presence and availability speak volumes for the Church, for the Franciscan Sisters, and for themselves.*

*According to the country's website, the Constitution requires that all children attend school until they achieve a basic level of education, which is expected to be nine years. However, the Ministry of Education reports that the average number of years that students spend in school is actually less than seven. The government pays for the cost of primary and secondary education, but parents pay additional expenses, such as fees and transportation. Unfortunately provisions for public schools fall far below the levels needed, and class sizes are often very large. In rural areas, only 10% of the children go on to high school.*

*Approximately 95% of Ecuadorians are Roman Catholic. Festivals and parades are typically based on religious celebrations, many incorporating a mixture of rites and icons.*

Our mornings were usually slow. One morning during the first week a lady with two children came to the door asking for whatever. She didn't know what she wanted. Someone had already given her food. She didn't want to leave.

The sisters started a day shelter for those

*Giving coffee to Carlos and Victor*

*Sara and Rosario giving Sister a sweater*

who were homeless or who had no food in the house for breakfast. They came for a cup of coffee, a piece of bread, and a half banana, and sometimes would stay for classes, such as reading, writing, and sewing. The sisters prayed that more money and more helpers would become available so they could add other classes.

Our evenings were very busy. We regularly visited the dining room where up to eighty people were fed each day. We visited the soup kitchen. I should say I visited, while Sister Ramona prayed, sang, and studied the Bible with the poor. Or we would greet members at the weekly Alcoholics Anonymous meetings, but more often we would join Bible study groups.

Bible study is a sign of faith. Usually it was a group of women who gathered to study the Bible and to share ideas. For example, the Maita family, usually twenty people including children, gathered to listen to the Word. There was something spurring them on – maybe Sister Ramona's presence. I don't think it was content.

The Bible group at Anita's house had a different class of people. These were educated people living in a well-furnished, clean house. Bible study was reflection more than study. These women had a good understanding of what was happening in the country as well.

Bible study up the hill with the Sosa Family included only two women from the family and two women catechists. They were learning about the Bible, but applying it to their daily lives was missing.

The second week I started tutoring some kids. Poor things! The schools were overcrowded, making it difficult to learn, especially since there were few books and supplies. Some children were up to the fifth or sixth grade and didn't even know the alphabet. There was no way they could learn to read. Three kids, fifth grader Jonathan, third grader Miguel, and first grader Estefania, came to our house for tutoring. They could say the alphabet in order, but did not recognize the letters out of order.

*With Jonathan, Miguel, and a visiting priest*

Maybe the children were just slow, but I'm sure a few suffered from fetal alcohol syndrome. One little girl was so dyslexic, she not only did everything backward, but also upside down. There wasn't much hope for

*Jonathan and Miguel and alphabet bingo*

these students as there were no special classes or testing – not even special attention such as individual help from the teachers. They're just passed on from grade to grade. Most often they get too far behind the other students, and drop out of school.

It seems those able to learn did so, while those who had a hard time became outcasts. But for those who could learn, the phonics that was taught in the lower grades was very good. I made alphabet bingo cards for the kids. Sister Ramona invited four kids from the same family to play bingo. They didn't know the names of the letters at all. It didn't pay to play. It was more entertaining than teaching.

The Catholic Church seemed to be quite conservative although they have Basic Christian Communities, charismatic prayer groups, Bible study, and John XXIII groups. Priests were quite clerical and somewhat authoritarian. Both priests and sisters were put on pedestals by most people. Although lay people did many things, it seemed they were not given real leadership in the church.

During the month I attended several churches in Duran. The churches here were so different. The sound system was bad. If fans were used, it was breezy. If the wind was blowing, it was breezy too. Most of the walls were decorative cement blocks covered with chicken wire to keep out the birds.

The priest, Padre Vicente, at Iglesia Virgen de las Mercedes in El Cerro de las Cabras, was good with the kids. But he had only the little ones. Mass was mainly for children and the elders. A few young couples attended. The bigger ones and youth didn't come anymore. I wondered why. There were no lay leaders to take over. Padre Vicente and Sister Ramona took the lead. In church everybody sang with heart and soul, and with lots of voice – meaning very loud.

One Saturday evening, there were a few young girls, a couple, about ten older women, two men, but mostly children attending

Mass in El Cerro. There were as many parts harmony in the singing as there were people at Mass. It was more like yelling than singing. It was pretty bad. Generally the singing was pretty good, except loud and throaty, but there were not enough adults at the service.

*With Padres Vicente, Francisco, and Vinicio*

At Sunday morning Mass, the singing had total participation. Actually it was very good singing, in their terms. Maybe there was not quite total agreement on key, but there was no agreement on tempo, except for the Ave Maria which was sung or said at every Mass just before the final blessing. That was beautiful. Everyone sang together and harmonized.

I visited another church, Iglesia del Senor Misericordia (Divine Mercy) in Gilberto, with its white-painted bamboo walls. There were benches, about eight inches wide with no backs, to sit on. This little church was packed. There were too many people for the few priests and sisters. The church could not flourish that way. Not many people received Holy Communion, and no one received in the hand. They believed that one must go to confession before receiving Communion.

One week I attended a Vicariate Meeting. On the agenda were reflections by Padre Veraldo, leaflets for the pastoral group, criteria for the counsel of the social pastoral group, vocation week, jubilee year, and pastoral ministry to the family. The questions and problems in the Catholic Church are the same all over the world – pastoral, charity, and social action problems. Should we give to everybody who asks? What about a second collection? Are there too many extra collections? Should we have open dates for meetings or special functions? And so on.

Our Saturday routine included lunch with the priests – usually the pastor, Padre Francis, and three very young priests. They were friendly and easy to talk to. We often had ceviche de camarones (shrimp), but there was other seafood in it too.

I visited the hospital in Duran which looked like a place for anything but healing. Patients were lying on cots in their clothes. They brought towels from home, and were given sheets if they didn't have their own. Ants were running all over the bed stands. The only clean looking areas were the nurses' garments.

Recently five cases of AIDS were diagnosed just across the river in Guayaquil. The doctors and nurses didn't have any more needles to treat the dialysis patients but the procedure had to continue. One does not want to get sick there.

The clinic run by the parish looked a bit better, actually a lot better in comparison. The dentists' office had rather good equipment. The pharmacy seemed quite well stocked, much better than the public hospital.

I loved visiting the sick and elderly in Duran. Carmen Arias was 99 years old, almost blind, but had a sharp mind. We talked about her grandson in New York. I also visited Connie, an elderly lady who had a stroke some time ago. She has a daughter in Madagascar.

Two buses took us to evangelization in El Recrea, a settlement on government land. After a windy and noisy ride, it was a relief and a pleasure to

*Sister Kizzie with Carmen and daughters*

get there. El Recrea was quiet with no heavy traffic. The area was actually rather clean and had water, sewers, and electricity. The people appreciated our visit.

## A Difficult Economic Climate

*There was a national strike in 1999 during two of the four weeks that Sister Kizzie was in Ecuador. Beginning in 1997, a combination of factors, including el niño weather patterns, the sharp drop in global oil prices, and a decrease in the gross national product, precipitated the severe economic and financial crisis and national strike.*

The national strike caused great hardship. The government of Ecuador controlled everything, including teachers, police, army, doctors, and nurses. The government said that it had no money so no government worker received a salary for three months. During the strike, most of the social service people worked at least part time, but the schools were closed. Catholic and private schools also closed in sympathy with the public school teachers. But I think it was because teachers knew that it would not be safe for them to stay open. They or the schools most likely would have been stoned. I'm glad they closed because we lived on the second floor of part of the school.

When workers finally received a pay check and went to cash it, the banks had no money. They were told to come back at the end of the month and then were given only half the amount of the check. The hospitals and clinics had no supplies left to work with. It was said that doctors and nurses worked, but helped themselves to supplies and sold them.

Money was scarce and the currency, the sucre, was devaluated a bit more. It seemed the price of gas was going up, and was a controlling factor in whether the strike continued or not. The price of gas was up to 30,000 sucres – about $3.00 per liter which would be more than $10.00 per gallon in United States dollars.

The strike stopped all public transportation. Sister Ramona and I did a lot of walking in Duran. Guayaquil was across the river, only 15 minutes by bus over the four-kilometer bridge. I got to know Duran quite well, but not Guayaquil or the rest of Ecuador, as we had no transportation. Besides it would not have been very safe to go into the big cities. We felt very safe where we were in Duran.

During the second week of the strike, we were told not to walk up the mountain for Bible study. It would be too dangerous on the streets. There still seemed to be a lot of traffic in Duran, even though no trucks were coming from the mountains to bring supplies into the cities. The markets were open, but the shelves were nearly empty. We walked to the post office. It was closed because the postmaster had gone to Guayaquil for a meeting. There was no problem yet with us walking in that area.

Large cities such as Guayaquil and the capital city, Quito, had more riots, and some were vicious. There were demonstrations in Guayaquil against the president. It was not safe, especially for foreigners. The president of the largest bank was arrested and taken to prison. I didn't understand why or who took over.

One day we heard rumors of more trouble. Many of the indigenous had gone to Quito to march. Estimates were that there were 50,000 demonstrating in Quito. One block from our house, lots of mostly young men were blocking the street. It was a demonstration in Duran! I ran down to the street just as everyone else did to see what was going on. I couldn't see much, but I didn't trust getting closer. There were too many people in the way. Also, it would be easy to blame foreigners for the trouble. People were stoning the private cars driving on the streets. Apparently some cars had replaced the bus service. The violence didn't last long. The police came and disbanded the rock-throwing men. By noon Duran was peaceful.

Protesting the high gasoline prices, the indigenous living in the mountains cut and burned tires in the middle of the road to be sure no trucks would get through to carry food to the cities. Markets stood empty, a real hardship for many, as ordinarily people only buy food for a day or two at a time. Now there wasn't any food to buy. Besides many people were afraid to come out and walk the streets. Many asked us for food. We bought 100-pound sacks of rice and Quaker Oats and put some of these common foods into smaller plastic bags and passed them out. It's interesting what one can do with oatmeal. Have you ever tried a Quaker oatmeal drink? It's drinkable, especially with sugar and cinnamon in it.

No market meant no food for many. For me it meant that there was a little – just a very little less noise out in the street.

According to news broadcasts, the president intended to freeze gasoline prices. The news also showed many people demonstrating in the towns along the coast. The taxi and bus drivers, and their passengers, were fighting the police. They said they had just parked their vehicles and the police shot at them. At the same time, the news showed the market in Guayaquil full of produce and lots of people moving about freely and at ease. What a contradiction!

Thankfully after two weeks, the strike ended abruptly one evening. Buses and other public transportation started running immediately. But some workers lost their jobs; others were only paid sporadically. Many were ingenious at finding ways to make a few sucres. The sucre wasn't worth much, 11,940 to $1.00 on August 1, 1999.

*When Sister Kizzie left Ecuador in August 1999, the sucre was worth about 12,000 to $1.00. Later that year, there was more than a 50% increase in inflation and the sucre lost 67% of its* *foreign exchange value, dropping to 25,000 sucres to $1.00. In early 2000, Ecuador adopted the United States dollar as the country's official currency. The dollar became legal tender in March 2000, with the sucre exchangeable at Banco Central at 25,000 sucres per dollar.*

## Traveling in Ecuador

*Sister Kizzie had the opportunity to tour several places in Ecuador after the strike. Guayaquil, a city of more than three million people, is the nation's main port. The city is located on the western bank of the Guayas River, which flows into the Pacific Ocean near the equator. Because of its location, the city is the center of Ecuador's business and manufacturing industries, and the home to many beautiful churches.*

*Duran built on edge of Babahoyo River*

While the strike paralyzed all public transportation, Sister Ramona and I used this opportunity to walk in Duran to visit the sick, attend prayer meetings, and work with the Basic

*Houses built on stilts into the hills*

70

Christian Communities. I became very familiar with Duran but the rest of Ecuador was put on hold. It didn't make any difference as each day was filled with worthwhile experiences.

Contrary to the United States where the rich build their homes in the foothills and on the sides of mountains with the gorgeous panorama laid out before them, it's the poor in Ecuador who build on the sides of hills. On the steeper slopes, they build the front of the house on stilts so it is level with the back of the house, which sits on solid ground. Or a piece of hill may be carved away to make a flat spot on which to build. Even on the most crowded hills, the houses appear to be built better than many houses on the crowded hills of Nogales in Mexico. People are poor here too, although I saw no starvation.

Our house in Duran was about three or four blocks

*Ferry from Duran to Guayaquil*

from the Babahoyo River. The nice walk along the river is called the Malecón. This is the place to dress up and go strolling on Friday and Saturday evenings. The river does not have a beach. It rises and

*Canoe passing lechuga on Babahoyo River*

falls with the tide of the ocean – muddy and dirty at a low tide. At times, the sea weed or water lilies, called lechuga, float east and at other times, west. It's fascinating. We watched white birds with long necks sitting on the lechuga.

The public ferry leaves at regular times from the Malecón for Guayaquil. This smooth twenty-minute boat ride has beautiful scenery along the banks of Duran and Guayaquil.

One Sunday when we decided to visit Guayaquil, there were so many people waiting for ferry rides or just sightseeing, that it was easier for us to take the bus to Guayaquil. The trip costs 2000 sucres or about 20 cents, but only ten cents for seniors. Crossing the four-kilometer Duran Bridge by bus was scenic too.

*The Cathedral and Plaza Seminario*

Guayaquil is a big city with a lot of noise and traffic. I don't want to live there. Parque Centenario, the largest park, occupies four city blocks. With its large Statue of Liberty and trees arching over the walkways and lawns, the Parque is a breath of fresh air in the middle of a big city.

Another favorite spot is Plaza Seminario in front of the Cathedral with its fish pond filled with colorful Japanese tilapia. There are huge land iguanas here, a different species from those on the Gallapagos Islands. The tourists and locals feed them m a n g o    s l i c e s purchased from park vendors. That day, nine iguanas were

*Train with rhino engine*

out and about, begging for mangos. Including its tail, the biggest iguana was probably six feet long. It was resting on the sidewalk and people were petting it. The young iguanas were greenish in color.

We had dinner at the modern Grand Hotel. The prices were as American as the hotel; the buffet was about $7.00. The food was tasty and a good variety. I loved the mixed seafood ceviche, made with mostly squid and shrimp. We had a fifteen-minute train ride through the town in small cars pulled by a rhinoceros engine. It was well worth the 3,000 sucres or 30 cents. We passed the Church of Santo Domingo, the oldest in Guayaquil. It was founded in 1548 and restored in 1938. On our way home we stopped at a beautifully-maintained cemetery.

On another Sunday afternoon, after the strike, we accompanied a group of folks from Duran on a pilgrimage to visit seven churches in Guayaquil. We visited six – couldn't find the seventh. Mostly, a church is a church. But St. Thomas Aquinas Church, also called Coop Pancho Jacome, is unique. There is a baptismal font built in the floor in the middle of the church. When the font is open for a baptism, the candidate walks down the steps on one side, is immersed, and then walks up the steps on the other side. It was very symbolic. When the font is not in use, it is

73

*Church of St. Thomas Aquinas*

covered with five squares in the form of a cross. The entire wall of the Sanctuary behind the main altar is covered with a mural showing the birth of Christ, Christ as a Child, the Last Supper, and then the Resurrection. What a beautiful church!

The Nuestra Senora de la Alborada is a modern looking church which Pope John Paul II visited in 1985. It has a tabernacle in the center, a raised altar, and statutes of St. Joseph and the Divine Child. The workers in the church kept right on sweeping around the visitors. A sign near the door said, *"No conversar dentro del templo, es la casa del Senor, Lugar de oracion. Para entrar a lo casa de Dios vestir corectamente."* Translated in English it said: "Do not carry on a conversion in the church. It is the house of God. A place of prayer. To enter the house of God, dress correctly."

The Santa Isabel Madre del Precursor Church has a large health clinic and pharmacy. We couldn't get into the church.

We ended our pilgrimage at a Retreat and Conference Center named Santuario de la Madre Tres Veces Admirable de Schoenstatt, loosely translated as the Sanctuary of the Virgin Three Times Admirable Mother of Schoenstatt. Some ladies called it a Rincon de Paz – Corner of Peace in the middle of a big, busy, noisy city. Away from the traffic noise, sisters from Germany take care of the beautiful grounds with pots of ferns hanging from trees, many flowers, and places to walk in quiet and peace. There is a small chapel with the outside walls covered entirely with vines. The vegetation was lush; the air was fresh; and the Presence of God was evident. It was a beautiful ending to a beautiful day.

*Corner of Peace Chapel*

On another day we had a memorable trip to the beach. Posorja is a small village of 15,000 people more than two hours by bus from Duran at the delta of the Guayas River. In the past the village's main occupation was fishing. Because of new high-tech fishing methods and the sea's high pollution, the unemployment rate was now more than 50%. Some of the people had part time work in the village's three fish processing factories.

The retreat house, Casa de Nazaret, had only three sisters and a small school for about a dozen young kids from the neighborhood. Unfortunately the sisters could not keep up the place. Groups didn't come anymore. They would have to make many changes so the place would be more welcoming to visitors.

It was cold and windy on the beach. Nevertheless there was much to do and see. I picked up platilla del mar – big sand dollars. On the bus ride home, we saw banana plantations, grapes, black vultures, trees with yellow flowers and no leaves, donkeys, pelicans, ocean liners, sailboats, and a cactus which looks like a cholla. We were intrigued by the savo tree which looks as though it grows upside down. Its branches and trunk are greenish. It has tiny leaves, and flowers only once a year. The balls hanging at the edges of the branches are filled with a cottony fiber which is used for pillow stuffing.

That day we learned some new vocabulary. A sign in the bus read, *"En caso de mareo, pide una funda."* *Mareo* translated is car sick. *Funda* is plastic bag.

On our way by bus to Cuenca on another day, we passed acres and acres of banana plantations with plastic wrapped around the hands of bananas. We saw palm trees, sugar cane fields and irrigation, but mostly on Dole Plantations.

Rounding a curve, the mountains came into view. It was like going home to Peru! Clouds covered the peaks. These mountains are at an altitude of 6,000 feet, and the Altiplano is at an altitude of 13,000 feet. Even at a lower altitude, these mountains appear to be less populated than in Peru. But the fields appear to be better taken care of and are greener, although we saw only those along the highway and not those in the hinterlands.

Indians much like the Aymara were working in the fields and along the roads. Some came on the bus. Their actions are so much like those of the Aymara. I felt right at home.

Unfortunately I got car sick from riding the bus into the altitude with so many curves. Although I missed some scenery, I slept a bit to keep from seeing and feeling the curves.

Cuenca is the third largest city in Ecuador. In 1999, it was declared the outstanding planned Spanish colonial city in the Americas and named a World Heritage Site. Cuenca was cold, very cold for us. We stayed at a retreat center with the sisters, three from Spain, one from Colombia, and one from Cuenca. They couldn't have been nicer to us, giving us lunch and showing us to our rooms.

I was still not feeling well from the bus ride, but went into the city to visit the Cathedral, the flower market, and the local market. I ate little supper. The next day I was in bed all day with diarrhea and the chills. I only had tea all day. We were glad to leave the next morning. I didn't eat so I could handle the bus trip back. Dramamine helped and we made it home safely. Thank

God! I had a piece of toast and then went to bed.

Unfortunately that was not the end. The next week was pretty much the same. When even a half piece of toast was too much for me to handle, I went to the clinic. The amoeba can sometimes be stronger than the human body. I would hate to do battle with them often. I was put on antibiotics. The next day, I had the first tiny hunger pain.

## Returning Home

I brought a colony of amoeba or whatever they're called home with me from Ecuador. They do not make very good guests. They may be small but they are very powerful. First, they didn't let me eat. Then later they couldn't be satisfied. They rechewed everything I ate until it was liquid and ran right through me. They sapped every bit of energy that I had. The medication I got in Ecuador did little or no good. Now that I am home and have stronger medication, I'm on the mend, and winning the struggle with the amoeba. I've warned them not to come back but was given no guarantee as the eggs have ways of hiding in the crevices of the intestines.

Now at home, so many questions linger. Are we just rich Americans who have much and should just give everything away? Does that teach others to beg? Will the people always be dependent on others? The questions tear at the heart of missioners. The answers are so complicated.

*Part One*

# Part Two
# United States/Mexico Border

One does not need to cross borders
made by people to divide countries.
The borders have become much more subtle,
invisible right within our own cities,
towns, and rural areas.
Sister Kizzie, 1986

*A few years after leaving the high altitude of the Andes Mountains in Peru, Sister Kizzie relocated to Arizona. Her mission experience in South America, her strong command of the Spanish language, and her love for helping those in need led her to the United States/Mexico border. So for more than twenty-five years she has taken on many challenges and roles in southern Arizona – teaching, ministering, supervising, and volunteering with various groups, including young students, the homeless, battered women, the sick and homebound, the Tohono O'odham Nation, and the migrants.*

*Stories of Sister Kizzie's first fifteen years on the border are found in Part Two. These stories describe the chaos on the border, her year with the Tohono O'odham Nation, and her work with BorderLinks, a binational organization which leads educational delegations to Mexico. Stories of Sister Kizzie's next ten years with Humane Borders are found in Part Three.*

*In 2005 I spent a month working with Sister Kizzie at Humane Borders digitizing tapes of news events and documentaries. Viewing these tapes, visiting inland and border cities in Mexico, and going to the desert gave me a personal perspective and better sense of the complex, conflicting, and chaotic border issues.*

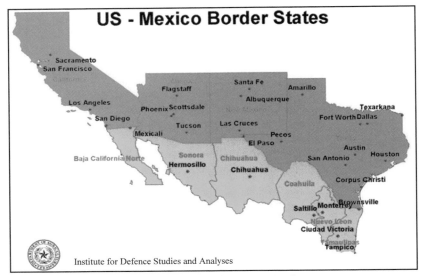

## US - Mexico Border States

Sacramento
San Francisco
Flagstaff
Santa Fe
Amarillo
Los Angeles
Phoenix Scottsdale
Albuquerque
Texarkana
San Diego
Tucson
Las Cruces
Fort Worth Dallas
Mexicali
Pecos
El Paso
Austin
Sonora
Chihuahua
San Antonio
Houston
Baja California Norte
Hermosillo
Chihuahua
Corpus Christi
Coahuila
Brownsville
Saltillo Monterrey
Nuevo León
Ciudad Victoria
Tamaulipas
Tampico

Institute for Defence Studies and Analyses

*Nearly 2,000 miles of United States and Mexico Border*

*Everywhere I went in Arizona and Mexico, I saw the challenges and rewards of Sister Kizzie's service and her commitment to the poor and oppressed. Sister describes what it means to cross the border.*

## Crossing Cultures

Crossing cultures means crossing a political border and being with people who either are of another race, another language, having different customs and beliefs, or are just different from our way. Crossing cultures used to mean working in a foreign country. Now one does not need to cross borders made by people to divide countries. Within our country there are many people who have settled from other countries, just as our ancestors did a few generations ago. The borders have become much more subtle and invisible right within our own cities, towns and rural areas.

The 2,000 mile border between the United States and Mexico is the longest land border in the world between a third world country and a first world country. In one step of crossing the border, it becomes immediately apparent that there is a difference. The years I lived in Peru with the Aymara people gave me the experience to easily move into another culture and to help others become acquainted and comfortable with another culture.

## Chaos on the Border

*Today the smuggling of illegal drugs, money, and weapons across the United States/Mexico border are of great concern to both countries. A decade ago when Maria and Pedro migrated to the United States, illegal immigration was the primary border concern.*

*"I only want to find work to take care of my family." Maria left her five children with her mother in Honduras and for five months walked and hitched rides across our border. In the United States she found work in a slaughterhouse but was often taken advantage of because she did not have a work permit. Her dream of a better future was in reality a nightmare. She worked at least ten-hour days with only short breaks and sometimes received only half of her expected wages. Her fear of being deported or fired kept her working several years until she injured her arm trying to lift a heavy load. Maria had no workers' compensation. A year later, she was still jobless, living with help from former workers.*

*Pedro, a Guatemalan, arrived in the United States after crossing through the Arizona desert. He found work on a farm, sending part of his $80-a-day earnings to his wife and children in Guatemala. The majority of his earnings is used to pay off his $7,000 debt to smugglers called coyotes. He lives in fear of being detected and deported.*

*In 1992 there were an estimated five million undocumented workers in the United States. That number has more than doubled in less than twenty years. Reports now estimate that there are between eleven and thirteen million undocumented workers in the states.*

*Sister Kizzie spoke about border issues between the United States and Mexico in Little Falls, Minnesota in 2001.*

## An Imaginary Line Which Unites and Divides

Thank you for the invitation to speak about a place where two worlds meet, where within a few minutes, one can go across a specific point and feel as though transplanted, not only into a different country but onto a different planet.

I would like to introduce you to this border area which I have called home for some time.

First, a little about borders in general. The word border has been defined in many ways and exists in many areas. We sometimes refer to this United States/Mexico border as a line between a first and a third or fourth world, or between a developed and developing nation, or between two different cultures or two different countries. No matter what word we use to define it, the line has been set by someone.

The first time man looked at the earth from space and saw the entire globe at one time, man detected no boundaries between countries. Borders exist only where we have put them, sometimes detectable and sometimes very difficult to detect.

I had experience walking across the imaginary line between countries. Once as I was hiking in the mountains between Peru and Bolivia, I was able to find the imaginary line marked by three-foot posts about 20 meters apart. I zigzagged across this line on purpose, about fifteen times, just to say I crossed without having my passport checked. No one cared.

About two miles from where I was hiking was an official road crossing with an archway and patrols on each side making sure only those with legal papers crossed. Someone cared.

The same was true along the United States/Mexico border until recently. While I lived on the Tohono O'odham Reservation, I could cross into Mexico – into another country while never leaving the tribal land and no one cared. The O'odham land is one portion of the 2,000 miles of United States/Mexico border. I point out this particular stretch of land because it is becoming the hot spot on the border right now.

The imaginary line has become much more prominent. Imagination is no longer needed to mark the spot. At first, chain links and barbed wire fences marked the dividing lines. Then walls were put up in the cities. The United States Marines just finished constructing a twelve-foot wall in the Douglas-Agua Prieta area, lengthening it at least two miles east and west of the cities. The same had been done in Nogales a few years ago and in California prior to that.

The Border Patrol

*Migrant footprints in Buenos Aires National Wildlife Refuge*

83

explained that the marines were doing the construction work, saving money by not hiring private companies, and that they were using the material from the temporary airstrips which had been used in the Gulf War. They carefully point out to us that the government is concerned about recycling.

*Immigration, we read, is primarily driven by the economic imbalance between the United States and the countries of Mexico and Central America. The devaluation of the peso in late 1994 threw Mexico into economic turmoil, and subsequently into the worst recession in more than fifty years. The crisis left a large segment of the more than 100 million people unemployed or underemployed, and approximately half of the population living below the poverty level. In many areas, people were literally starving to death. Sister Kizzie has had first-hand experience.*

## No Job and No Land

There are many folks from many countries coming across the border, but I have contact mostly with the Mexicans. I'd like to tell of some of my encounters and give you some idea of why they would want to leave their homeland. A man told me that he and his family were starving so, knowing of the dangers of crossing the desert, he decided to give it a try. He said, "If I don't go, my family and I will starve to death. If I go and die, I will be just as dead, but I will die knowing that I tried."

In Mexico he lived in an agricultural area and could grow enough for his family to live on. Big companies from the United States bought much of the arable land, promising the people they would have work. They did, but only for a year. Then the big machinery came in. The laborers were no longer needed. Now they had no job and no land. Some were forced into the mountains where farming is very difficult and nothing grows well. I have seen men working on the sides of mountains hoeing their crops. They don't bend over to hoe because the slope is so steep. You can imagine what happens when it rains. In one area corn did pretty well and they would use that as a cash crop. Then corn was imported from the United States and sold cheaper than they could sell theirs, so they lost their cash crop. Small farmers in the United States are experiencing the same situation.

Another man told me that he has a wife and two children to support. He had worked in a factory until the United States economy took a downturn. The factory closed and moved to another country where labor was even cheaper. Now he had no work and they were starving. He had to take his chances.

*Since the 1994 North American Fair Trade Agreement (NAFTA), huge corporations have taken over farmland and replaced laborers with machines. Families who had farmed for generations making their living by raising and selling seed corn no longer had the means to make a living. Truckloads of corn were now transported across the border from the United States for large growers to purchase at a lower price, leaving no market for the small farmers' corn.*

Small businesses as well as small farms collapsed. Local factories closed their doors as they could no longer compete and remain profitable. Factories were burned to the ground. The news media reported that an estimated one million manufacturing jobs and one million farm jobs have been lost since NAFTA.

International businesses had been operating across the border employing many Mexicans because labor was inexpensive. But when companies discovered that they could find cheaper labor in China and the Philippines, many closed their factories and relocated. They gave no warning to workers, no pay at the end of the week, and no severance pay.

*At the same time the United States had a rising demand for low-skilled labor and a shrinking labor force willing to do the work. For example, migrants were willing to take jobs in agriculture, meat processing, landscaping, and housekeeping, which typically pay three times what they would make at home. That is, if they could find work in their home country.*

*And so, stories abound of the woeful plight of migrant workers in search of higher paying jobs to support their families and communities. Most migrants do not come to our country to harm anyone. Mostly they are the young, strong, healthy, and ambitious who migrate. They come to work despite the fact that they are often exploited, intimidated, and paid less than United States citizens for the same job. Unfortunately the demand for counterfeit documents such as social security cards, driver licenses, and resident-alien green cards has skyrocketed. Fraudulent documents became readily available and fairly cheap, making these the rule rather than the exception.*

*In 1996, after Sister Kizzie had been in southern Arizona for about ten years, she found herself in the midst of these immigration issues. She wrote the following article for the October 1996 BorderLinks publication, Loaves and Fishes.*

## To Respond or Not to Respond

A woman cried out and pleaded, but to no avail. She was ignored. So she continued pleading and crying out because she knew her cause was important and urgent. The woman was a Syrophoenician, a stranger, a foreigner to the Jews at the time of Jesus. Jesus ignored her. At the insistence of the Apostles, he finally spoke to her and said, "First, let the children eat all they want, for it is not right to take the children's bread and toss it to the dogs." Mk 7:27.

Jesus was limiting his ministry and his healing power. Not

only did he say he wasn't sent to help her, a foreigner, but he insulted her by referring to her as a dog, a very derogatory term.

It appears that the United States also finds ways to ignore, offend, and make immigrants – foreigners, feel unwelcome. The latest move on the part of the United States Congress was to pass a measure denying most federal benefits to non-citizens during their first five years here, and social security benefits to most legal immigrants who haven't lived and worked here for ten years. It seems the children will be hit the hardest. Who did Jesus mean when he said, "First, let the children eat . . . ?"

The measure signed by the president states that immigrants do not qualify for federal assistance even in a personal crisis. Maybe it should also say, "Since we won't help you, you need not pay taxes."

There is no such indication. Should the immigrants feel the tax burden while we refuse to respond to their needs? Are we being fair and just?

Not even when the Syrophoenician was highly insulted, did she walk away. She spoke up using the words of Jesus. "Sir, even the dogs under the table eat the crumbs." Mk 7:28.

Who knows if Jesus was surprised at her response, or happy, or angry. It makes no difference. He reacted positively and even commended her for speaking back to Him.

"For such a reply ... " He acknowledged her pleas and granted her request, which was the healing of her daughter.

How are we going to respond to our president and to legislators? Or will we respond at all? How are we going to respond to immigrants, whether legal or not, who come into our country? Are we going to say that we have paid our taxes – only to care for ourselves?

Or will we be like Jesus and say, "You have great faith. What you want will be done for you." Mk 15:28.

Do we have the faith it takes to react to the measures taken by our governmental leaders? To speak up for our voiceless neighbors? To recognize faith in others? To follow the example of Jesus and live the Gospel message? To carry the universal standard set by the United Nations General Assembly in 1990? The standard expands the definition of the rights of immigrants to include not only people fleeing political persecution but also those who are dislocated as a function of natural disasters and abject poverty.

Besides the Syrophoenician woman, many throughout both the Hebrew and Christian Scriptures have crossed borders. To note but a few. In Leviticus we read that aliens who have crossed over to live in the land should be treated as native born. Lev 19:33-34. Ruth, the ancestress of Jesus, crossed geographic, religious, ethnic, and cultural borders for love of another. Book of Ruth 16-17. The Good Samaritan, a member of a foreign and enemy people, took a risk by extending his hand. Lk 10:29-37.

All through the ages, people have crossed borders. As most citizens, I am in the United States because my ancestors took the risk of living in a foreign country. Would I be alive today had they not done so? What are the possibilities that my mother and father would have met had not her grandparents, who were born in Germany (or was one born in India?), and his parents, who were born in Slovenia, immigrated?

Most of us could ask the same questions. Are we ready to reclaim the powerful moral and biblical imperative to welcome the stranger in our midst?

*With the closing of the United States border in 1994, migration moved from the urban crossings to remote areas. Arizona's border, which is about 350 miles of the border between Mexico and the United States, is made up mostly of desert and mountain ranges. Because of today's twelve-foot-high fencing, vehicle barriers, bright spotlights or high-tech surveillance* devices on 80% of the Arizona border, migrants cross through the deadliest regions. They risk exposure in the desert, having their money stolen, and being raped, kidnapped, or beaten by bandits and smugglers. They risk death by dehydration on what could be an eight-day walk across the searing Arizona desert.

No where is the fencing more evident than in the border town of Nogales in Sonora, Mexico about sixty miles south of Tucson. A fifteen-foot high wall of Army-surplus steel lines the border. On the Mexican side of the wall are crosses depicting the migrants who have died in the desert. Other artists have depicted the struggles of life on the border with both white and colorful icons.

*Crosses on the fence in Nogales*

The artist, Alberto Morakis, says his sculptures can be viewed in two different ways. On the Mexican side, the figures look as though they are trying to push the wall down. On the United States side, the figures appear to be holding up the wall.

*Art depicting the life of the migrant*

*Holding up or pushing down the wall?*

*Art by Alberto Morakis*

I saw the huge cost of immigration when I visited the desert. Land owners, visitors, and environmentalists are alarmed by the huge amounts of trash left behind by migrants. There is not enough rain to restore the devastation to plants and wildlife caused by the large number of vehicles creating new roads. Only in time will we know how the fences impact the environment, and how migratory patterns of animals such as jaguars, ocelots, bear, cougars are disturbed. In more than ten years, all we have done is relocate the areas where migrants cross the border.

## The Plight of the Migrants

Many migrants who arrive in our country do not reach gainful employment. Border Patrol and other law enforcement catch and return migrants every day to various locations across the border in Mexico.

In Nogales, Mexico we visited the border shelter run by the Kino Border Initiative named after a Jesuit priest, Padre Eusebio Francisco Kino. Padre Kino started the San Xavier Mission on the Tohono O'odham Reservation in southern Arizona more than three hundred years ago. Today the Kino Border Initiative works with migrants and studies the effects of migration along the border. The Initiative also educates the people about Padre Kino and promotes his sainthood.

The border shelter was built by the city of Nogales about 500 yards from the Port of Entry. A sign on the fence lets travelers know about the shelter. The Jesuits run the program, feed, clothe, and give medical aid to migrants. On the average, 200 deported migrants, mostly men, are fed and helped daily. Many have leg and foot injuries from walking through the desert. Waiting at the shelter, migrants are given a variety of chores. We saw men at a table peeling and cutting vegetables. In the back, men were washing dishes.

*Shelter for deported migrants across the border in Nogales*

*A few blocks away we visited a home for women and children who have been deported. The sisters give them food, clean clothing, and a temporary place to stay until they can rejoin their families.*

*Visiting a home for women and children*

In June 2000 Sister Kizzie wrote about the migrant's plight for the BorderLinks publication <u>Loaves and Fishes</u>.

The problem of illegal immigration is rooted in Mexico's ongoing economic crisis and the complex relationship between the United States and Mexico. Adding to the problem are the smugglers (coyotes) who lie and exploit the migrants.

In San Diego, border control was gained by the Border Patrol, shifting the migration eastward into Arizona. The migrants are crossing by the thousands each day in the desert areas away from the cities. The death toll is rising daily as the heat and dryness of the summer increase. The Border Patrol has successfully diverted flows from the cities into the countryside and that is dangerous territory. More manpower and equipment are not the answers.

Many local groups all along the 2,000 miles of land border are responding to the plight of the migrants. Here in Tucson a group called Derechos Humanos, which means Human Rights, organized a Vigil for Peace. This was in protest of migrant issues as well as vigilantes who have taken it upon themselves to be the law. Approximately 300 people met at sundown for the candle light vigil to pray, sing, and hear speeches.

Another group is meeting and reflecting on the situation in light of our faith. It was decided that some immediate action is needed, such as water stations at strategic spots in the desert for the migrants. We will work with several other groups from California and Washington, D.C. to promote the long-term need of policy change.

*Poster offering aid to migrants*

The Tohono O'odham Reservation is the deadliest migrant trail in the United States. The Native Americans are by nature hospitable people but the increased presence of the Border Patrol has made it difficult for them to do more than just give water and food to the migrants.

*One cannot help but think about the migration perspective from the Mexican side of the border. We visited Altar, a meeting city in Sonora, Mexico for migrants from Latin America and other parts of Mexico. A community leader told us it breaks his heart to see the immigrants cross the border to the United States. The best resource Mexico has – its human capital – is leaving the country in droves. In addition Mexico has a lot of productive lands which now are barren.*

*The human costs of migration are staggering. Immigrants who gain employment in the United States have wives, children, and parents still living in Mexico. They live with fear that they will never see them again. For more than a century people have passed back and forth across the border with relative ease to visit family, to work, and to purchase goods and materials. Before our border policies changed, migrants came for seasonal work and then returned to their homeland. Now the increased security has made the crossing very difficult. Once undocumented migrants are in the United States, they cannot go home. Instead they send money to their families, which is often used to pay for them to come to the states. The result is that we have permanent undocumented residents at a huge social and economic cost – boredom, isolation, and depression with increasing alcoholism, burglary and crime.*

*In 2004, Sister Kizzie gave the following talk at Our Mother of Sorrows Church in Tucson.*

## Missed Opportunities

Migrants and migration have been a part of United States history for as long as we know. Maybe even before we can remember. The American Indians, who were here before the Europeans, might have migrated from other areas too. There are so many theories. Many of us came from immigrant ancestors. It is a part of American history as well as world history.

Migration has not been spoken about as much until recent years. It may be due to the large number of migrants coming to the United States or more likely due to the number of deaths. Many migrants died right here in our state, or as I recently began saying *in our backyard.* Or it might be because so many groups are making a public issue of it and bringing it to the attention of the governmental officials and the nation.

I can't say that I paid a whole lot of attention to immigration until I started working at BorderLinks in 1995. We frequently went across the border to Nogales, Aqua Prieta, and Ciudad Juárez. We visited the maquiladores and were very concerned about the workers and worker rights, but not the migrants.

Now I wonder why I didn't give it more thought. I worked with migrants in 1976 in the Red River Valley along the Minnesota/North Dakota border. But then it was different. These migrants came every year. They were invited. They knew they had a job when they arrived. And when they finished their work, they went home.

I didn't work in the sugar beet fields with them, but I was working for the Catholic Church. We had religion classes and I gave the homilies because the priests didn't speak Spanish. But mostly I spent my time preparing the children for First Communion.

My concern then was not for the migrant worker, but the relationship of our churches in Minnesota with churches in Texas and Mexico where the migrants came from. With us the children made their First Communion in a month or six weeks. At home it took several years. When they returned home, they would not attend religion classes anymore because they already had made their First Communion. The churches in the south were not happy.

The other problem we faced came from the local people. The government was paying the public schools for the use of their classrooms and for buses to take the migrant children to the neighboring town for swimming. The local children could not get on the bus even if they offered to pay for the ride. This did not help the relationship between the two cultures. What opportunities we missed.

## Seeking Common Ground

*In Altar we were given a copy of a Guide for Migrants written by the Mexican government. It looked like a comic book, but elicited a very serious debate. The guide warned migrants about the dangers of the desert. It told them to follow power lines if they get lost, to put salt tablets in their water to avoid dehydration, not to run or use weapons if stopped by the Border Patrol, and to avoid behavior that would attract the attention of law enforcement.*

*Supporters called it a survival guide. Critics called it a guide on how on illegally enter the United States. Supporters say the Mexican government has taken responsibility in warning the migrants of the dangers in crossing the desert. Critics say the government is not discouraging illegal immigration.*

*The Mexican government has responded in other ways, particularly to drug smuggling. Drug cartels in Mexico control the major flow of foreign narcotics into the United States, representing a multibillion dollar business for Mexico's mafia. Since his election in 2006, President Felipe Calderón called for an international approach to drug use and drug trafficking. He has taken action against the country's organized crime.*

*Yet drug and gang violence continues to increase in Mexico. Criminal gangs do what they can to protect their lucrative smuggling routes for money, drugs, guns, and migrants. The reported death toll is staggering – nearly 40,000 killed in Mexico in the last five years. Many of these deaths occurred very close to our border. It's not surprising that warnings about traveling to Mexico appear everywhere in the United States.*

*In November 1998, Sister Kizzie attended the meeting of the Human Rights and Social Communication Organizations in Cuernavaca, Mexico. Other countries, including France, Germany, and England, were represented as well. The purpose of the meeting was to analyze the relationship between civil organizations of Mexico and United States so as to increase communications, trust, and coordination.*

"We are learning to dance, not getting married. We represent a different kind of globalization, one which has roots in the people. There are many from every country voluntarily putting effort and energy into global unification. So we continue to dance together, to learn from each other, and to cooperate as brothers and sisters to create a better world." With these words, one of the organizers, Emilio Alvarez-Icaza, opened the conference.

Everyone came willing to share personal and observed experiences. Though no one had any preconceived ideas of what the outcomes might be, all those present were motivated by the same ideals – those of peace and justice. The organizations from each country described their political, economic, and social situations. Their goal was to join hands and strength and power to work together for the good of all.

Representatives from the United States openly spoke of human rights violations within our country. We raised questions about NAFTA, as well as other issues. Other participants seemed a bit surprised that those of us from the United States were willing to question and admit that not all is well in our country. That we also have problems. That we too have injustices. The reality became apparent, and dissolved a tension that had been permeating the atmosphere from the beginning of the meeting. We were very willing to admit that we all have the same problems and they affect each other. No one country alone can protect or save itself or any other country. There has to be cooperation. All must work together for the common good of all.

After several days of discussions, both countries saw the need to develop a common agenda that would support and strengthen both sides. The following points were suggested as focal.

First, militarization. What is the main objective?

Second, democracy. How can folks from both sides be educated concerning the economic question, "Who is being helped for what?"

Third, human rights. How do we strengthen our influence among other organizations in each country?

Many challenges were verbalized. Who are we? How are we helping each other across borders? How do we communicate and how can we communicate more effectively? How do we reach the majority of the people? How do we understand ourselves better? There is a need to strengthen our forces, and encourage other groups. There is no reason that one country should question the other on issues of justice.

Many conclusions were drawn from this binational meeting. We have great responsibilities to each other. We need to unite forces. Various groups having the same objectives should meet more often nationally to better understand and encourage each other. We should divide the work among the groups nationally, have a conference concerning border issues, share an agenda and its implications among organizations, and gather more information about NAFTA.

This was a very exciting conference in which we came together as brothers and sisters to work for the good of all.

*Over the years major proposals have been put forth in the United States by the president, legislators, Homeland Security, humanitarian groups, and others to reform immigration laws, toughen border security, and institute guest-worker programs. The recent passage of Arizona Senate Bill 1070 (SB) represents the latest immigration crackdown.*

*The reality is that it doesn't matter where we live in the United States. We are all involved in the immigration issues. From the food we eat to the homes we purchase, we have all benefitted from undocumented labor. Whole industries such as farming on the West Coast, meat packing in the Midwest, chicken and turkey processing in the South, depend on immigrant labor. With our high unemployment today, it's not clear whether illegal workers have been replaced, or would be replaced even if employers offered higher wages.*

*Humanitarian groups all over the country call for nations to work cooperatively on economic development in the migrants' home countries. Border fences won't stop illegal border crossings because they don't address the poverty and desperation in the countries of origin. They are just another obstacle to desperate people. While it appears that no immigration legislation will be passed by Congress in the near future, others are not resting on their laurels. More and more volunteer groups from across the United States gather to help in any way they can. Unfortunately vigilante and other hate groups and their activities have expanded as well.*

*United States lawmakers and citizens do not agree on whether immigrants contribute to our economy and to our society, but all agree that countries need to work together on this complex issue. A recent quote appearing on the Internet explains the difficulty: "When politics catches up with economics, there will be reform."*

*There is a successful coffee grower cooperative called Just Coffee which brings together coop members from Mexico and the United States. It has facilities in the neighboring border towns of Aqua Prieta in Sonora, Mexico and Douglas, Arizona. Just Coffee imports green coffee beans from many different areas around the world, including Mexico, Guatemala, Nicaragua, Bolivia, Peru, and the Dominican Republic. The coffee beans are roasted as far north as Madison, Wisconsin. The pure organic Arabica coffee is sold through church groups, special events, and through the Internet.*

*Think of what a coop could do with Just Tequila!*

*Part Two*

## The Tohono O'odham Nation

*Formerly known as the Papago, the Tohono O'odham Tribe is a group of aboriginal Americans who reside in the Sonoran Desert of southwest Arizona and northwest Mexico. The Tohono O'odham, whose name means People of the Desert, lived in this region for centuries. Their rich history and culture continue to thrive today. The O'odham retained their customs and still speak their native language.*

*In September 1994, Sister Kizzie was introduced to the O'odham Nation. After living on the Reservation a short time, she wrote the following article for the Franciscan Sisters' Community Newsletter.*

### One With the People

Pisinimo – a new word, a new village, a new people.

Pisinimo – at the edge of the world, or a little beyond.

Pisinimo – isolated, desolate, the southwestern area of the Native American Reservation in Arizona.

Pisinimo – home of the Tohono O'odham, a nation as foreign to us as distant lands and far away countries.

Pisinimo – now the home of Sister Ange Mayers and Sister Elizabeth Ohmann.

Once it becomes home, it will no longer feel new or strange or distant. Five days are not long enough to become acquainted with the people but we are making a start. We have already been introduced to four of the nine or more villages where we will minister. The people are friendly in a quiet and shy way. Conversations, meetings, discussions, classes – all have many periods of silence – a comfortable silence. It's a time to become acquainted by being present for each other, a time for reflection and contemplation.

Already I had some new experiences. A palomino horse jumping our fence and eating leaves from branches as high up the ironwood tree next to the church as it can reach. Dogs following us as we walk the streets. Participation in a one-year anniversary prayer service and a meal. A dust storm so heavy it was impossible to see the neighbor's house only half a block away – carrying the top sand to the west and blowing in new sand and dust. Rains that empty the clouds in one hour causing the roof to leak. The evaporative cooler blowing hot instead of cool air. A visit from the district manager welcoming us. Curious children wondering what the new sisters are like. Wild horses coming to the corral for water close to our house.

There are many things to learn, and adaptations to make. Mostly we are concentrating on becoming one with the people.

*Since its creation, the Reservation has held the remains of their ancestors and is considered sacred territory. The O'odham love nature and feel responsible for the land. Sister Kizzie described the symbolism found in a patch of weeds to the Franciscan Community.*

## A Patch of Dark Green

Even though we were still in the boundaries of the United States, living with the Tohono O'odham Nation was like living in a foreign country. We had to adapt to a whole new culture, language, and way of life.

The Native Americans love nature and would like to live off the land. As they say, "God created the land for us to use and to care for. God is present in all parts of nature."

In one field which was just turning green after God gave it a good drink of water, there was a patch of weeds in the form of a cross. This was a very dark green. God was telling us that He

101

was present there.

But this filled the people with a lot of questions. Was that cross there to remind us of God? Were we not caring for this field as God expected us to? No one ever answered these questions, but they did stir up a lot of thinking.

*The Tohono O'odham Nation is recognized as a sovereign government by the United States and Mexico. With a land base of 2.8 million acres, it is one of the largest tribes in the United States. Their lands are divided into four different districts. The largest is Sells, the Nation's capital, which extends into Mexico. For more information about the Tohono O'odham, please visit their official website at www.tonation-nsn.gov.*

*In recent years, the Nation's nearly 80 miles of the United States/Mexico border has become a barrier for the O'odham. Their members must produce passports and border identification cards to travel through their own traditional lands. They cannot freely visit family or sacred historic sites on the other side of the border. They cannot freely transport foods and materials, including their cultural and religious items, such as feathers, pine leaves or sweet grass. After several hundred years, our immigration laws now prevent the O'odham from freely practicing their religious,*

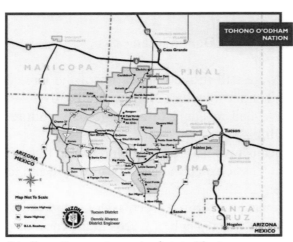

*O'odham Reservation extends into Mexico.*

*economic, and cultural traditions.*

*The Nation has nearly 28,000 members living both on and off the tribal lands. At any given time, there are approximately 14,000 citizens on the Reservation, with about 1,500 on the Mexican side. Since tribal leaders have steadfastly refused to put up a physical fence to stop others from crossing, there could also be thousands of migrants on their lands as well. Because of the Nation's extremely high unemployment rate, drug smugglers have successfully hired the O'odham to work for the cartels. For example, they have offered up to $1,000 for the O'odham to drive a car an hour or so across tribal lands.*

*In an attempt to stop illegal smuggling, the Department of Homeland Security set up mobile substations and a detainment center on O'odham land. It uses unmanned surveillance airplanes and helicopters, and numerous vehicles including jeeps, hummers, ATVs, and dirt cycles.*

*The Nation sees itself as a victim of the United States war on terrorism. It is here that Sister Kizzie worked for approximately one year. She wrote the following article for the Franciscan Sisters' Our Journey in 1995.*

### Pilgrims become One with the People

Originally living off the desert, the Tohono O'odham naturally moved as necessity required. In the summer, taking advantage of the hot weather and rains, the O'odham lived on the desert floor caring for their crops. After the cold set in, the O'odham took refuge in the hills or mountains which provided them with wild animals for food.

In time this land, an area of 2.8 million acres, was declared a Reservation for the Tohono O'odham, and now belongs to the Nation. The people no longer journey from desert to mountain with the seasons. Villages have been established around what originally were the summer living sites, depending on the availability of water.

It is in nine of the villages on the southwestern end of the Reservation that I walk with Sister Ange Mayers and the Tohono O'odham. As pilgrims we journey the same paths in the villages as the O'odham travel. A pilgrim belongs to the people and comes into the lives of others. As two pilgrims among these Native Americans, we sit with, listen to, and speak with them to discover who they are and how they struggle. We try to be available as friends who sit down and are willing to wait until the other is ready to speak.

As two pilgrims, we meet people face-to-face who have lost a son through a stabbing. We meet people face-to-face who are unwilling to meet or speak to their neighbors because of an age-old feud. We accompany Jesus to a house where an elderly or sick person is housebound. We discuss the responsibilities and privileges that parents and godparents take upon themselves at the initiation of their child into the Church at baptism. We offer sympathy and compassion to families who have lost a member through an alcohol-related accident. We support people in their sobriety sometimes accompanying them to Alcoholics Anonymous meetings. Village and district leaders often come to share their ideas, their programs, and work – including both the progress and frustrations.

As pilgrims, we try to become one with the people with whom we journey. At times becoming one gets quite homey, for example, when the family dog accompanies the family into the church and lies at our feet during Mass. Depending on the time of year, I was thankful when the dog would lie at my feet to keep them warm. The churches are unheated and very drafty.

An important time for the O'odham is at a wake which usually begins with the funeral Mass and then lasts all night. Food is served continuously. Choirs from all around the Reservation take turns singing hymns and praying the rosary. Burial takes place early the next morning.

As pilgrims we follow an ancient prayer tradition and set out on a pilgrimage journeying beyond our present place to a holy place. At times our pilgrimage destination is a church in a neighboring or a distant village. The farthest village to which we minister is 36 miles during the dry season when the gravel and dirt roads are passable. Otherwise, it is 55 miles. At such times we modern-day pilgrims use the convenience of a car as our mode of transportation.

As pilgrims and missionaries living in a strange and foreign culture, we realize we are temporary residents. Our focus, therefore, is to empower the people to become leaders and take the responsibility of ministering to each other and considering themselves as the Church. A Scripture-based reflection group, called Builders of the Earth, meets weekly to prepare the O'odham to become Eucharistic ministers, prayer leaders, readers, song leaders, church caretakers, and other church leaders. Some participate for their own personal growth. Leadership empowers people to take ownership of themselves and the Church.

In return, we also discover who we are and where we are going. A pilgrim's heart is challenged to be open to others.

## Mission San Xavier del Bac

*A second land base of the Tohono O'odham is San Xavier, just south of Tucson. Located here is a personal favorite – the Mission San Xavier del Bac or White Dove of the Desert. Because the underground Santa Cruz River surfaces near the mission, it is also known as the place where the water appears. The mission is surrounded by cotton and grain fields with hills and mountains in the distance.*

*Main church with unfinished tower*

*Mortuary Chapel at the old cemetery*

*This Spanish Catholic mission was founded in 1699 by a Jesuit missionary, Padre Eusebio Francisco Kino, who often visited and preached in the area. The current church was constructed by the Tohono O'odham and Franciscan priests in the late 1700s.*

*Many legends exist about the unfinished tower of the church. One is that early taxation laws exempted buildings which were under construction.*

*This beautifully preserved mission attracts people from all over the world. After extensive restoration of the interior and exterior, the church now appears in its original state. Today the Franciscans serve the Native American community, celebrating daily Mass in the main cross-shaped* church or in the Juan Diego Chapel. San Xavier parish has the oldest parochial school in the Diocese of Tucson.

*Chapel of the Sorrowful Mother*

In an ornate wooden box in one alcove of the church is a reclining statue of the likeness of Saint Francis Xavier, the patron saint of the mission.

According to legend, if one can lift the head of Saint Francis off the pillow, one is free of sin and in the right standing with God. If one can't lift the head, that person should examine his

*Roy lifting the head of Saint Francis*

or her conscience to see what they have done before God.

## BorderLinks

*Sister Kizzie left the Tohono O'odham Nation in 1995 to work with BorderLinks located in the city of Tucson. Started in 1986, BorderLinks has become a vibrant combination of community center, think tank, conference catalyst, micro-enterprise innovator, and educational tourism bureau. For more information, please visit their website at www.borderlinks.org.*

*According to cofounder Rick Ufford-Chase, the ultimate vision of the organization is to build bridges across borders, not only between the United States and other countries, but to build bridges across the borders of misunderstanding, suspicion, and hostility that may be based on historical experience but have divided people too long.*

*In 2001, Director Ufford-Chase wrote a tribute to Sister Kizzie in celebration of her fiftieth anniversary as a Franciscan Sister. It was reprinted in <u>Loaves and Fishes</u>, a publication of BorderLinks.*

## One in a Million

This summer Sister Elizabeth Ohmann, who has been a BorderLinks staff person since the fall of 1995, will celebrate fifty years as a member of the Franciscan Sisters of Little Falls, Minnesota. For those of us at BorderLinks, that celebration will be bittersweet, since Sister Elizabeth has let us know that she'll be leaving BorderLinks as well. Now in her late sixties, one might expect that Sister is looking for a chance to rest, but given her life of service and commitment to the community, I know that it is far more likely that she'll look for another vocational challenge.

Sister Elizabeth was in many ways the bridge between the old BorderLinks and the new. During the spring of 1995, I told many people that the perfect person to help BorderLinks grow and to help us model the diversity and ecumenism I knew we were called to, would be a progressive thinking, Spanish speaking, Catholic Sister who had worked in Latin America. In the early fall of that same year, it was a surprise even to me when Sister Elizabeth showed up and met all those expectations. With her willingness to take a chance on a small group of young Protestant volunteers on the border, she earned my undying appreciation and gratitude.

Sister Elizabeth thought of the details when no one else did. She identified the problems we were having as we began to grow and could no longer depend on the informal encounters to communicate with one another. She brought order to chaos and forced us to slow down and to think carefully about the choices we were making. She made BorderLinks' first inroads into the Catholic Church that have allowed us to become truly ecumenical on both sides of the border.

Perhaps more than anything else, Sister Elizabeth has been a mentor to me and to more than a dozen others who have worked at BorderLinks over the last six years. In her lifetime, she has been a teacher in at least six schools, a missionary in Peru for almost ten years, an administrator in schools and retreat centers, and a pastoral care provider in the Native American Community in southern Arizona. At a time when she should have been slowing down, she took a job with a bunch of twenty-somethings leading intensive educational seminars for BorderLinks. No one will ever leave more of a mark on our work. I for one expect to see her legacy each day for as long as I work at BorderLinks.

Thank you, Sister. You truly are one in a million.

*Sister Kizzie summarized the work of BorderLinks for the* <u>*Catholic Vision*</u>, *a publication of the Diocese of Tucson in 1996.*

## Life in the Gap

In this our changing world, gaps continuously widen. In southern Arizona on our border with Mexico, the gap between the first and third worlds meets. We live within this gap. Faced with issues from both sides, we are in a strategic position to learn about and to examine the impact of these issues.

To realize this potential, BorderLinks was born. The origins of BorderLinks date back to the 1980s when volunteers to the Sanctuary Movement became convinced that there was a need to help people visit the border in order to educate them about Central American refugees and their concerns. Since then, the focus of BorderLinks has broadened to provide North Americans with an understanding of the many complex issues on the border.

BorderLinks is an ecumenical program designed to raise consciousness about these issues through experiential education. The staff designs and facilitates seminars, ranging from one day to three weeks. Based on the educational philosophy that the best educators are those people most affected by the issues, a seminar includes extensive time in Mexican communities.

Interviews with governmental officials, business managers, church leaders, community leaders, social service providers, factory workers, human rights and environmental advocates may include free trade, the environment, and social and economic justice.

On a BorderLinks trip, we believe in giving participants the opportunity to listen to many perspectives, especially to voices that are not often heard. The stay in a Mexican community with a family provides an opportunity to build personal relationships with border residents who are struggling to improve their communities. Each trip begins with a meditation on a Scripture passage and ends with analysis and reflection of the day's experiences in relation to that Scripture and our lives.

We encourage participants to see the reality of divisions and separations within their own cities in the light of the reality experienced on the border.

All Christian people believe that the social dimension of the Gospel is integral to their faith. The Catholic Church faces a major evangelization challenge to raise awareness of the link between faith and public issues.

## Educational Delegations

*A key part of the work of BorderLinks is the educational program. More than a thousand people from the United States participate each year in seminars, which typically number from ten to thirty people and last from a day to several weeks.*

*In 2005 I joined fifteen mostly retired people on a one-day educational trip with BorderLinks to Nogales in Sonora, Mexico. First we toured the new business area. Since NAFTA, about a hundred United States businesses set up modern factories called maquiladoras in border cities like Nogales. These maquiladoras employ thousands of Mexicans, paying the minimum wage which at that time was about $45 a week for a 48-hour work week. Women need to work too, so young children are often left unattended for much of the day.*

*As we looked across the city, we could see homes creeping up the hillsides. Mexicans identify a location for their homestead, live on that site often in a cardboard shack for a few years, and then have to seek permission from local government to build a permanent home. Unlike in the United States where building a home and living at higher elevations are very costly, in Mexico, the higher up the hill, the poorer the residents. The reason, of course, is that there are no water or sewer systems, or other city services at higher levels.*

*BorderLinks uses an economic tool to compare the equivalent price for a worker in the United States if the buying power would be the same as in Mexico. For example, if we take a typical food item, such as a gallon of milk, it would cost about 30 pesos in Mexico. If a Mexican worker earns 10 pesos an hour, he or she has to work three hours to pay for a gallon of milk. In the United States if a worker earns $7.00 an hour, the equivalent price of the gallon of milk would be $7.00 times three hours or $21.00. How do Mexican families survive?*

111

*In 1998 Sister Kizzie wrote about the growth and legal status of BorderLinks in the Franciscan Sisters' Community Newsletter.*

## Can Borders Dissolve?

BorderLinks believes that the best teachers are those right on the border who live the issues. Whenever we lead a group on a seminar to Mexico, we invite folks from various organizations on both sides of the border to speak to the group participants.

Often if the trip lasts more than one day we arrange home stays. Host families invite us to eat, spend the evening with them, and sleep there. Many times this means throwing a sleeping bag on the floor. Most of the host families are also refugees of a kind. They have moved north to the border to work in the factories also known as maquiladores because they could not make a living in central or southern Mexico.

After seeing and hearing much on our seminar border trip, we reflect on the situation. How does this affect us personally? What will we do with the information when we go home?

When two others and I came to BorderLinks nearly four years ago, the staff increased from four to seven. In October of last year we had another big jump from seven to eleven. This was of monumental significance for us as three of the new staff are Mexicans. Before we could hire Mexicans, we had to become a civil organization giving us legal status in Mexico. It took almost three years to understand what was needed and to do the paperwork.

We are now indeed binational, both as an organization and as staff. Has the border between here and Mexico really begun to crumble? Maybe not, but maybe the one rock out of the wall, or on the border shall we say the one link out of a chain-link fence, would weaken the entire structure. Jesus is the link between God and humanity. He would like to be the link to replace the entire chain-link fence.

Our hope is that as more participants share the realities of the border, they will return to their homes and cities and see their own realities in a different light. Not only cities, but rural areas as well, have walls and borders built right within. Many ethnic groups, socioeconomic groups, slums, and the homeless have walls built around them. Why have these invisible walls been built? Is it to keep them out of our space, or is it to keep us out of their space? Is it fear of people? Fear of one another? Or fear of the unknown?

"You cannot think straight with a heart full of fear, for fear seeks safety, not truth. ... A heart full of love, on the other hand, has a limbering effect on the mind." William Sloan Coffin

*Delegates are encouraged not only to form relationships, but also to think critically about how their lives have been changed by the experience. In the Franciscan Sisters' Community Newsletter in 1997, Sister Kizzie wrote about the change in the meaning and outlook of her life following a BorderLinks trip.*

## Hope for the Future

Several weekends ago my coworker Katie Glynn and I led a group of Jesuit volunteers from Phoenix on a BorderLinks trip into Mexico. These volunteers were young ladies in their early twenties. It was heartwarming, encouraging and hopeful for the Church to see such highly motivated and dedicated young people. God is very much alive in the world.

For two days we visited health promoters, governmental officials, immigration agents, environmentalists, social workers and many others who work in the maquiladoras and live in the colonias – neighborhood settlements which grew as work became available. We listened, questioned, and reflected on the information presented to us.

The last afternoon we wandered the streets, visiting with vendors, shop owners, or whoever would take the time to speak with us. We checked food prices to make comparisons between the buying power in Nogales and the United States. Translating the costs to working hours, we calculated that it takes a maquiladora worker more than three hours at minimum wage to buy a gallon of milk. Working the same number of hours at minimum wage in the United States would put the cost of a gallon of milk at approximately $20.00. That changed our perception of work in the maquiladoras.

Sharing a meal, conversation, and spending the night with a family in a cardboard house in a colonia is not an experience soon forgotten. Sharing when there does not seem to be anything to share is a true mark of hospitality. Somehow there is always something to share.

The last afternoon with our van packed with sleeping bags, backpacks, and supplies, we crossed the bridge back to Nogales, Arizona, breathing a sigh of relief that we had encountered no challenging situations. Our last visit was at the museum with a woman who had dedicated her life working for the rights of the people living in the colonias. With her permission we left the van in the museum parking lot while we walked back across the border for dinner at a restaurant. We wondered what it was like to own a business in the economy which we had experienced in Mexico. Unfortunately the owner was not at the restaurant at the time to answer our questions.

Crossing the border back into Arizona after the wonderful dinner and conversation, our moods were positive. Arriving at our van, our moods quickly changed. The window on the passenger side had been broken and three backpacks were missing. Since we were on the United States side of the border, we notified the police. While waiting for the police, one of the young women and I walked around the block to check garbage cans.

"Maybe they only wanted money and threw the backpacks away." No such luck.

As we walked the young woman remarked, "Yesterday we spoke about being attacked. Today we saw people with very little leading happy lives. Now is our opportunity."

I admired her, but at the same time felt violated. There was not much of any value taken. My backpack and camera can be replaced. However, the film inside cannot be replaced.

After such an experience, there was no way to return to our daily routines at home and at work as we normally did. The meaning and outlook of life had truly changed.

*The next story highlights a growing problem – alcoholism. Sister Kizzie wrote the following about accompanying a group of seminarians on an enculturation trip to Mexico.*

## Go Home and Sleep It Off

We spent several days in Hermosillo, about sixty miles south of the border. Some families gave us hospitality and a place to spend the night. Several seminarians were up early and went for a walk. I sat in the front yard waiting for the day to begin. It wasn't long before the seminarians came back, very excited and afraid. They told me they had been attacked by two men.

"Wait a minute. Tell me what happened before we start accusing them of attacking." I said.

The men had asked the seminarians for money. Since none of the seminarians could speak Spanish, they became a bit agitated and finally understood that the men wanted money. One seminarian had three pesos – about 30 cents. That apparently didn't please the men.

No one could explain how they reacted, but it scared the seminarians. They came back in a big hurry. We talked about it in the front yard. Within minutes the two men came down our street. I asked everyone to just stay sitting and I would talk to the men.

The group was afraid and did not want me to go and talk to them. I told them not to worry. By that time I could tell that the two men were drunk. I again asked everyone else to stay back. I walked to the middle of the street, greeted the men, and asked if they had talked to some members of my group. They said they only wanted money. I had a little talk with them about the hospitality of the neighbors around here and they should not spoil that kind hospitality. Then I asked if they had been drinking. They admitted that they had been drinking the evening before. I added, "And all night."

Then I explained that I was a madre and why we were visiting their city. The minute they heard madre, one took my hand and kissed it. The other got on his knees and said he was sorry. I suggested they go home and sleep it off.

As I turned around to go back to the group, I saw six seminarians in a semicircle about fifteen feet from me. They all looked so scared. Finally one found his voice and said, "That was impressive. What did you do?"

"Nothing really. I told them they should go home and sleep it off."

## Humble Hospitality

On a BorderLinks trip I accompanied a group of seminarians from various denominations to Hermosillo, Mexico where we would spend the next five days. Arrangements had been made with host families to give us lodging, so we thought. On arrival our host showed us one room with one double bed on a dirt floor.

I felt many eyes on me, questioning, "What are we going to do?"

I explained to our generous host that there were fifteen of us and the floor space here was only enough for five sleeping bags. "Was there any other space?"

She thought for a moment and said, "There is a storeroom in the back, but it is not very good."

Immediately I knew her *good* and my *good* were not the same. "May I see it?"

It served us just fine. The neighbors across the street realized our predicament and offered us another room. Even those participants who had never been exposed to such dire and primitive conditions were willing to give it a try when they realized that I was willing to throw down a sleeping bag and share the humble hospitality of our host family.

## Experiencing the Border

*In March of 2003, an eleven-member delegation from St. Mary's Parish in Melrose, Minnesota traveled to Nogales, Mexico for five intense days with BorderLinks. Even though Sister Kizzie was no longer with BorderLinks, she participated in the delegation, which included Sister Janet Kunkel, originally from Melrose, and Sister Adela Gross. Sister Adela, currently coordinator for*

*Sister Kizzie and Sister Adela*

117

*multicultural ministry for the St. Cloud Diocese, spent many years with Sister Kizzie on the Altiplano in Peru.*

What happens during a BorderLinks trip? The first day the group from Melrose heard from a variety of speakers, including a historian and a representative from the Immigration and Naturalization Service. Reverend John Fife, pastor of Tucson's Southside Presbyterian Church for 31 years, talked about the

*Listening to a BorderLinks spokesperson*

origin of the Sanctuary Movement in the 1980s which helped refugees of the civil war in Central America. In 1982, Reverend Fife became the first pastor in the nation to declare his church in Tucson a sanctuary for refugees. He says there is no legal or moral justification whatsoever for developing a strategy that costs the lives

*Sister Kizzie explaining her work*

*Discussing the Mexico experience*

of hundreds of the poorest and most desperate people. To be poor and desperate should not be a crime.

The second day we went to Nogales, Mexico. At the border, the Border Patrol explained

*Enjoying lunch with the delegates*

their work and mission, and answered questions about border security. Then participants visited a maquiladora which manufactures electronic components. The manager answered questions about economic development in Mexico and gave a tour of the plant.

Families living in a squatter's settlement or colonia were the hosts for the next two nights. As the delegates slept and ate with their families, they learned much from those suffering oppression and poverty.

Educational delegations always include time for discussion

119

*Melrose Delegation. Back row: Joe Timmins, Sister Kizzie, Sister Adela Gross, Lupida Patrick, Emily Beette, Mary Gebeke, Robert Doyle, Madre Irene from BorderLinks. Front row: John Stokman, Irene Braun, Peggy Stokman, Lynn Klaphake, Carol Timmins, and Heather Craize from BorderLinks*

and reflection. Group meetings reflecting on the feelings and images of the experiences were held over the next two days.

The last day BorderLinks facilitated a number of exercises designed to analyze and reflect on our experiences. What does all this mean for us? What do we do next? How do we respond? What do we take home from this experience?

Unfortunately I work with BorderLinks trip participants for only a very short time. I am not able to follow through with them and their life transformations which occur because of their experiences and new relationships formed on the border.

## La Casa Misericordia

*Since BorderLinks became a civil organization in Mexico, it had the right to purchase property across the border. In 1999, the organization purchased a community center called La Casa Misericordia in Nogales. In 2000 Sister Kizzie wrote about this center in the <u>St. Cloud Visitor</u>.*

This past year BorderLinks has become a binational organization giving us legal status in Mexico as well as in the United States. I believe we are the only group doing this work organizationally across this border. With this standing we are able to hire Mexican staff, which we immediately did, making us also a binational staff. We work together as one.

Our legal status in Mexico opened another door. We were given the opportunity to purchase a community center called La Casa Misericordia. All the programs already there would continue, such as a hot lunch for about 350 children of the neighboring communities whose parents work in the factories which have grown up along the border. The group called Arco Iris for troubled youth holds retreats at La Casa Misericordia. Catechists have weekly religious instructions for the younger children.

*Sister Kizzie with some children*

*Part Two*

*With Janet and Sister Kizzie at La Casa*

On one visit to La Casa Misericordia (Mercy House in English) I was with Sister Kizzie, my aunt Janet, and Sister Audrey Jean Loher, a Franciscan Sister who lives in Tucson and works with border issues. Upon arrival we met a group of students leaving for the United States after three weeks of classes and work. The center regularly hosts educational seminars for international students.

Responding to community needs, La Casa Misericordia provides a food cooperative, clothing bank, and an internship program. It offers educational opportunities for Mexicans including English classes, guitar classes, after-school tutoring, a bike repair shop, and clubs for chess, crafts, poetry and theater. It has workshops on various topics, such as soap making, composting toilets, and alternative building techniques using recycled newspapers and tires.

*Sawdust in the bathroom*

*Instructions for composting*

The restroom facility resembled an outhouse with a nice toilet seat and a pail of sawdust. *After relieving oneself, the instructions are to sprinkle sawdust, which is then used as compost. Nothing goes to waste here!*

*Children in a classroom*

We visited the day care and the kitchen, which serves up to 350 meals to children each day. These are children from the neighborhood and the neighboring communities whose parents mostly work in the factories and don't get home until evening.

*Lunch in the day care*

Because there are too many for all day, the children are in school on a split shift, some in the morning and some in the afternoon. With the parents gone all day, most of the children have no place to go but roam the streets and eat whatever they can find.

*Waiting for a ride home*

*Volunteers help serve lunch each day. We ate with the older children in the lunchroom – beans, rice, noodles, tortillas and watermelon. The food was tasty and spicy. The amount we paid for the food will help the center buy food for the next day. Food in Mexico, at least in Nogales, costs about the same as food in the United States.*

*In 2010, the BorderLinks Newsletter reported that La Casa Misericordia reorganized into Hogar de Esperanza y Paz (HEPAC). HEPAC still offers educational classes, serves healthy lunches for approximately 300 to 350 children per day, and provides a safe haven for at-risk youth. In addition the Women's Cooperative, a model of economic sustainability for women in Nogales, makes and sells jewelry as a source of income for the women and HEPAC.*

## Past Experiences Never Past

Past experiences and learning are never past, gone or forgotten. When I was at BorderLinks, a group of Bolivian children was touring the United States performing their native dances. A contact person in Tucson asked BorderLinks if the children could be housed there for a few days.

The contact person and the Bolivian leader came in person to make arrangements. While walking across the parking lot to show the visitors their sleeping quarters, I asked the leader if he was Aymara or Quechua.

"Aymara," he replied and asked if I ever heard of them.

I responded with something in Aymara. He stopped dead in his tracks, looked very surprised, and then said to his companion: "She speaks Aymara!"

Then he laughed and laughed and could not believe he would ever meet anyone in the United States who could speak Aymara. It made him feel comfortable and at home.

# Part Three
# Humane Borders

"Give a cup of water in My name."
As a Franciscan, a follower of St. Francis of Assisi,
I tend to go where there is a need,
where the poorest are,
regardless of the dangers or risks involved.
Sister Kizzie, 2001

*In November 2010, Sister Kizzie received the Volunteer of the Decade award from Humane Borders for her dedication and extraordinary contribution to the mission of saving lives. At a reception with friends and relatives, she accepted the award on behalf of the countless migrants and more than 15,000 volunteers who make up this humanitarian organization which she helped start in 2000.*

*Part Three describes Sister Kizzie's work with Humane Borders. It includes the organization's support and volunteers, its relationship with law enforcement, dangers and deaths in the desert, and lastly, its advocacy for immigration reform. Please refer to their website at www.humaneborders.org for more information or to receive a Newsletter.*

## The Beginning of Humane Borders

*The story of this interfaith, nonprofit organization began in 2000 when approximately a hundred people met in Tucson to discuss the increase in migrant deaths in the Arizona desert. The recent death of one young woman named Yolanda Gonzales Garcia captured the hearts of many people. She died after giving the last of her water to her infant. They were found by a Tohono O'odham female police officer. Miraculously the infant survived.*

*The group included Rick Ufford-Chase of BorderLinks, a Quaker, David Perkins, Reverend Robin Hoover of First Christian Church, Sister Kizzie, and members of other organizations and churches from the Tucson area. Sister Kizzie wrote about the Pentecost Sunday meeting in her Christmas letter to family.*

A new millennium, a new year, some new involvements. That has been my experience this past year. My latest project is to help start a new organization called Humane Borders. Last June one of the Quakers, David Perkins, came to BorderLinks to talk to us about deaths in the desert. "We, as Christians, need to reflect on this from a faith perspective, and then do something about it."

David, Rick Ufford-Chase, and I decided this was too big a situation for the three of us. We needed more minds. David proposed that we have a meeting according to the Quaker method. We would begin with a query, think, speak about it, and allow the Spirit to lead us. Each of us called ten people we thought would be interested, and they could invite others.

On Pentecost Sunday, the interfaith group met and addressed two primary questions. How can we respond with compassion to the migrants who are risking their lives crossing the border? How can we affect the immigration policies which place these persons at risk in the desert?

After much discussion, we recorded eight points. First, because people were dying from dehydration, we would place water in the desert. The second point was to significantly challenge the migration and enforcement policies. Third, our logo would include the Big Dipper and the North Star. Fourth, the organization would become an umbrella group for interested parties. Fifth, our steering committee would include people from various churches. Sixth, the group would work binationally with Mexico as soon as possible and as cooperatively as possible. Seventh, this would decidedly be a faith-based organization. And lastly, we would use national and international media to tell the story of the plight of the migrant.

*Thus, motivated by faith, the stated mission of the newly created Humane Borders was to create a just and humane border environment. Its main objective was humanitarian – to save lives of those dying from dehydration in the desert.*

*Humane Borders has taken the position that they must not test* the United States laws or perceptions of the laws as they work to accomplish their goals. They would offer food, water, medical help, phone calls to authorities, and emergency transportation only if they notify the authorities. All actions and decisions would be public, transparent, open, and within the bounds of the law.

Along with food and clothing, we put out our first gallons of water on December 12, the Feast of Our

*Blue flag visible in the desert*

127

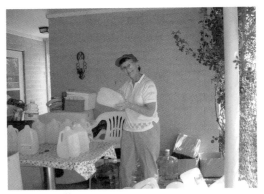

*Filling endless water jugs*

Lady of Guadalupe. Being the only Catholic on the team, I thought this was most fitting. We marked the water with a blue flag on a thirty-foot pole which can be seen from a distance. The very first day, more than half the water was taken. Hopefully we will save a few lives.

We are doing all this publicly and in the open. This has given us great opportunities to meet with Border Patrol, Immigration and Naturalization Service, the Mexican Consulates, and many other agencies and church groups. By working together, we can all move forward.

Jesus became part of the human race. We want to help Him make everyone feel a part of that one people.

*In the Fall 2001 issue of Our Journey, Sister Kizzie explained the motivation in organizing Humane Borders to the Franciscan Sisters.*

## A Cup of Water

"Whoever gives a cup of water to drink, as a follower of Christ ..." These are the words of Jesus. Mk 9:41.

"People are dying in the desert." This was reported by the Border Patrol of southern Arizona. This was reported by the police of the Tohono O'odham Nation.

I, along with 96 faith-filled people gathered in June 2000 to reflect on these statements. This reflection led to the birth of Humane Borders, an ecumenical, nonprofit organization with the goal to save lives.

*Sister Kizzie setting up a water station*

Our first action was to put water into the desert to save the migrants from the brutal death of dehydration. We began by putting gallons of water under a blue flag on top of a thirty-foot pole. Now we use 55-gallon drums which we refill each week and check for purity. During the hottest and driest season, the water usage can be up to 400 gallons each week.

This summer of 2001 has been most deadly. More migrants are being forced into the desert of western Arizona because security has become tight in urban areas. The heat and drought are so severe that no one can carry enough water to walk the miles of desert land. A walk to feed one's family has become a walk into a death trap.

Illegal immigration increased significantly in the late 1990s. Previously migrants came to find work to earn money to buy food for their families, or to find a better life. Then they returned to their families. More migrants are choosing to remain in the United States as it is too difficult to travel back and forth. They remain here and often bring their families.

Reading the Gospel can be a dangerous undertaking. "I was thirsty and you gave me to drink. I was a stranger and you welcomed me." Mt 25:35.

What did Jesus really mean?

*Part Three*

*Logo depicting humanitarian assistance*

*With Sister Helen Ann Klepaida at a station*

*Fully-equipped trucks ready for a desert run*

*The logo has the name Humane Borders printed in English and Fronteras Compasivas in Spanish. Depicting humanitarian assistance, the logo includes the Big Dipper, the North Star, and a drinking gourd adapted from the slavery abolitionist movement.*

*A water station consists of two 55-gallon polyethylene barrels placed on a metal stand. The barrels are painted light blue to reduce the heat, to be recognizable, and to prevent algae growth. They are fitted with spring-loaded valves to reduce accidental spillage.*

*Each water station is marked with a blue flag on a thirty-foot high pole.*

*Blue, the color of water, is a definite contrast against the colors of the desert. Water is delivered to the station on a specially-built truck equipped with a large water tank, gasoline-powered pump, and hose reel. Each truck has food packs, first aid, satellite telephones, GPS devices, maps, tools, and other resources for the specially-trained volunteer driver.*

*Humane Borders installed two water stations at Organ Pipe Cactus National Monument in March 2001. An application to put water in the Cabeza Prieta National Wildlife Refuge was denied. Then in May of the same year the Border Patrol picked up a record fourteen dead migrants in the Cabeza Prieta area. These deaths startled southern Arizona and became the catalyst for widespread humanitarian efforts.*

## It's Not the Water

I am often asked if I am encouraging migrants to cross the border by giving water. It is not the water that is inviting them. Arizona water really isn't that good. Besides, in the desert the water gets pretty warm and doesn't taste very good. Warm water, even hot water, doesn't hurt anyone. We drink hot coffee, tea or water. It is better for one who is dehydrating to sip warm water than cold water. No, I don't feel that I am encouraging anyone to cross, but I do hope that I am saving a life. I hope I am giving that cup of water Jesus was talking about in the Bible, or the cup of water the Samaritan woman gave to Jesus at the well.

I also don't think this is the final solution to the issue of migration. It is only a band-aid. Band-aids don't cure, but they help. Our second goal is to encourage the government to initiate a guest worker policy. Many employers in the United States are inviting workers from Mexico because they can't find enough workers who are willing to do the work the migrants do, or who would do it as cheaply. With a guest worker program, migrants could come for a specific job or for a specific time limit, and then go back home. From what I have observed, most would want that. As the situation is now, most are choosing to come and stay because it is too hard to come and go. It takes years, up to ten sometimes, to request and receive a work visa. A supporter of a family can't wait ten years to earn some money. I pray and I will continue to work for a change in immigration policy.

Admittedly there is corruption in the Mexican government as there is in almost every government in the world. A change in the corruption in governments of all countries could change the way all people live.

*Sister Kizzie wrote about the first anniversary celebration and the success of Humane Borders.*

## After One Year

On March 7, 2002, Humane Borders celebrated the first anniversary at the first water station in the Buenos Aires Wildlife Refuge in the Sonoran Desert. A blue flag atop a thirty-foot pole visible for quite a distance fluttered above a 55-gallon water tank. Gathered at a water station were staff, the press, a member of the Tucson Board of Supervisors, and guests. To mark the event, the water was checked to be sure it was pure and drinkable. Water had to be added indicating that migrants had been there during the past week.

Humane Borders has seventeen water stations in the desert offering water to migrants who are traveling north seeking work. During the winter the water stations are serviced every week to ten days. Now that the weather is warming and soon to be hot, the stations will be serviced every five to seven days. More migrants travel during this time of the year and more water is required to prevent dehydration. Our hope is to save lives.

As Jesus said, "A cup of cold water given in My name ..." We add "... may save a life."

Last year more than 100 migrants died in the desert. Putting water in the desert is a humane act. This week another migrant died just west of Tucson. As yet, Humane Borders has n o t   r e c e i v e d permission to put water in that area. We aim to double the number of water stations available to migrants this year.

Humane Borders is   l o o k i n g   f o r volunteers to service

*First anniversary celebration at the Buenos Aires Wildlife Refuge*

water stations and to pick up trash dropped by the migrants. Donations are graciously accepted as well.

*Humane Borders gained international media attention during its first few years. It's had global media coverage in major newspapers in Mexico and the United States as well as in Canada, Sweden, Great Britain, France, Germany, Spain, Italy, Japan, Chile, and Nicaragua. Television and radio stations have given broad coverage within the United States, and internationally on Univision International, Telemundo International, and British Broadcasting Company.*

*I spent the month of January 2005 working with Humane Borders. My primary job was to create DVDs from VHS tapes. At that time there were about 150 tapes of varying lengths and content. Many were media tapes of their work in the desert.*

*Humane Borders had sixty water stations in the desert when I arrived in Tucson, and now has more than a hundred stations. They study maps provided by Border Patrol to find out where most deaths occur, and try to set up water stations in those areas.*

Governmental agencies have been most receptive in allowing water stations on public lands. Approximately 85% of the land in the state of Arizona is federal land. The rest is urban, private, or Arizona State Trust Lands. The Trust Lands produce income for public education usually from livestock and agricultural leases. Hunting and recreation are allowed on Trust Lands, but Humane Borders is not allowed to operate water stations on these lands. We cannot even look for deceased migrants or cross these lands to maintain water stations on other lands. Recently though, we have initiated talks with the lease holders rather than the government to place water on the Trust Lands.

With permission and encouragement from the government and landowners, we have water stations on public land in Pima County, Organ Pipe Cactus National Monument, Buenos Aires National Wildlife Refuge, Cabeza Prieta National Wildlife Refuge, Ironwood Forest National Monument as well as private land in Cochise County and Pima County.

*For the first ten years, the offices of Humane Borders were located at the First Christian Church in Tucson. Their trucks were parked in the church parking lot next to a storage shed constructed by volunteers. Near the church is a Migrant*

*Memorial Ramada dedicated to the migrants who have died in the desert. One wall contains a large scale death map, a marker board, a verse of Scripture, and lists of the names of known deaths. The covered shelter serves as a meeting place for staff, volunteers, visitors, and migrants. Families of migrants often stop by seeking information on their loved ones.*

*Do the migrants find and use the water in the desert? When Sister Kizzie returned to Minnesota during the summer of 2002, she found the answer.*

*In the First Christian Church parking lot*

*Television interview in the Ramada*

## There are People Behind the Water!

Humane Borders has been setting up water stations in the Sonoran Desert of Arizona with the hope of saving the lives of migrants coming across the desert. When suffering from thirst, one feels the body dry up and lose strength. This suffering in one person can make the heart of another swell with the feeling of a need to give. Many volunteers in the Tucson area have felt their hearts stirring on hearing of the sufferings felt by migrants trying to cross the desert in the summer heat.

While setting up water stations or replenishing water at existing stations, one wonders whether migrants actually find, use, or appreciate the water. The water disappears but we are not sure where it is going. My doubts were dispelled this summer when I visited Minnesota and Colorado. I was fortunate to meet and speak with migrants who have crossed; who have experienced excruciating thirst; and who found water in the desert placed there under a large blue flag by those whose hearts hurt because others suffered.

I visited a settlement of migrants in Long Prairie, Minnesota. Many of the migrants had crossed the border in the western part of Arizona. They asked if I was familiar with the blue flags and the water stations in the desert. I replied that I was and that I was a part of Humane Borders. Their eyes opened wide and they replied, "There are people behind the water!"

There could have been no better words of gratitude.

When I asked a migrant why he risked his life crossing the desert, he responded, "If I was going to starve *anyway*, I might as well starve *anywhere*." By crossing the desert, he felt that he was giving himself and his family one more chance at life.

In Colorado I spoke to a family from Peru. Several members had come across the border in early spring. They heard about the water stations, so finding them was a sign that they had reached the United States. They were assured that they were traveling north. They expressed their gratitude and blessings for those who are so kind as to provide water for the thirsty.

One group expressed fear of going near the water stations. They were afraid that they would then be followed.

*In the past migrants left notes at water stations thanking the people for the water. Sister Kizzie does not often meet or speak to migrants at a water station.*

It is only on rare occasions that we meet migrants at water stations. At one sight we were erecting a new station. We set up the tank, filled it with water, and had just raised the blue

*With a migrant at Yrena water station*

flag when two migrants came out of the desert. They had been told that they could find water under a blue flag. Seeing the blue flag indicated to them that we were friendly people.

One migrant had no water left in his jug and the other had only a few ounces. They were most grateful to find fresh water, not only to drink, but also to fill their caps and pour it over their heads to cool off.

## Many Sources of Funding

*Humane Borders' entire operation is run by donations and volunteers. As a 501(c)(3), the organization can now receive tax-deductible contributions. Parish congregations, denominations, corporations, individuals, and local county governments support Humane Borders. For example, Pima County, which covers about 125 miles of the Arizona border, has given $25,000 annually to Humane Borders to support its mission. The county allows volunteers access to its land, and together they work with the Global Information Systems to produce maps and other information. The county officials realize it is to their advantage* *to help Humane Borders in keeping people from dying in the desert. Their 2006 budget for recovering and storing bodies of border crossers exceeded $300,000. In addition, the volunteers save the county huge amounts of money by removing trash left behind by the migrants.*

*Each water station costs approximately $1,500 to maintain every year. Naming a water station is one way to bring in needed funds. Several water stations have been named for volunteers. Fundacion Mexico raised money to fund a water station in the desert and named it the Unknown Migrant Water Station.*

*The largest expense is driving the trucks back and forth in the desert. Trips to fill water tanks, pick up trash, lead delegations, escort media, deliver blankets and food, are costly. The cost of one day's worth of gasoline during the peak season exceeds $300.*

*Every dollar counts. Humane Borders raises money from the sale of jackets, bumper stickers, water bottles, caps, T-shirts, note cards with art work, and other items.*

*One weekend in August 2006, Sister Kizzie and Sister Audrey Jean Loher were invited by a Methodist Church in Apache Junction, Arizona to speak about the water stations in the desert. It was an unlikely source of funding.*

## Sidewalk Sunday School

What a fascinating idea – a Sidewalk Sunday School! This is a project developed by the Methodist Church. One side of a truck was cut open, rebuilt, and fastened with hinges on the bottom. When pulled down from the top, the whole side created a stage. The back of the stage, which is inside the truck, has built-in cupboards for storing supplies for teaching classes. A clothesline strung across the length of the stage is perfect for hanging items, such as charts and posters.

After class, the small folding chairs with canvas seats and

backs are stored inside. The stage floor is pulled up and again becomes the side of the bus, ready to move to another site.

During the past school year, 20 to 25 children studied the

*Truck rebuilt for a traveling Sunday school*

migration issue at this site. Their Scripture verse to memorize that week was, "I have spoken openly to the world. I said nothing new."

From their reflection on this passage, they concluded that all of

*Students gathering for class*

us must speak out on behalf of the migrants crossing the desert. Also from Scripture they learned that migration is not new. More important, they learned that migrants are people. Each one is our brother or sister, and we should treat them as such.

Instead of the children paying for the classes, a collection was taken up each week. At the beginning of the year, the decision was made as to what would be done with the money. This year they planned to help pay for the water which Humane Borders puts into the desert. They gave us a check for $500 for water stations. We were grateful. When migrants find the water, they too will be grateful.

*Part Three*

# A Multitude of Volunteers

*Numbering in the tens of thousands, volunteers from international groups, as far away as Denmark, Iceland, and Korea, have come to help Humane Borders. Each volunteer has a combination service and educational experience learning about border issues. Work projects vary – checking water barrels in the desert, sewing and repairing flags, picking up trash, and maintaining the trucks and equipment.*

*To give you an idea of the scope of Humane Borders, each year, hundreds of volunteers donate more than 25,000 hours servicing water stations; make 500 trips to the desert; drive more than 40,000 miles; and dispense more than 25,000 gallons of water. During the summer, Humane Borders' trucks go out daily to fill the water tanks. During the winter, they usually go out twice a week. Countless other hours are donated each year for seminars, educational events, fund-raising, mailings, and book-keeping and office work.*

*My first trip with Humane Borders in January 2005 was a road trip through the desert. On this clear day we could see the thirty-foot high blue flag in the distance – designating a water station. We stopped to chlorinate the water. We saw many signs where migrants had crossed the land.*

*Since the federal government owns most of the land in Arizona, migrants cross public land for most of their journey. In some areas, private land owners graze cattle. The trash left by*

*An unexpected adventure*

140

*migrants is a huge problem. Volunteers from Humane Borders go out to the desert on a regular basis to pick up trash left behind in the desert. Why? To preserve and maintain the beauty of the desert and environment, to preserve the archeological treasures, and to protect the health of animals.*

Picking up trash in the desert

*One of the rooms at Humane Borders holds a collection of personal effects which volunteers found in the desert.*

Dragging bags of trash with Sister Audrey

*The collection contains water bottles, clothing, pharmaceuticals, medicines, backpacks, baby bottles, diapers, books, bibles, hymnals, photos and personal documents, and large items such as bicycles with flat tires and baby strollers. Migrants leave behind things which get too heavy to carry. Or when they meet smugglers, they change into a set of clean clothes and leave everything else behind. These items are carefully examined to gather information about migration patterns, and too often are used to identify bodies.*

*Humane Borders assembles health kits with basic hygiene*

*This shawl was handmade for you by a member of our prayer shawl ministry. During its creation, we prayed and asked the Lord to give the receiver of this shawl many blessings of love and comfort. May this shawl always be a warm reminder that you are loved and cared for.*

*United Methodist Church*

*products, and collects sheets, towels, blankets, bedding, and clothing for distribution in Nogales, Santa Ana, and Altar in Mexico. United Methodist Church in Los Angeles sent a box of beautiful shawls to Humane Borders. Each unique shawl contains a written message of love for the migrant.*

## A Founding Volunteer

*Other than for a six-month grant from the Conrad Hilton Foundation, Sister Kizzie worked for ten years as a full time volunteer supported entirely by the Franciscan Sisters of Little Falls, Minnesota.*

*Through the years she has wholeheartedly participated in every Humane Borders project. One of Sister Kizzie's unique projects was to design the best blue flag. From the beginning she sewed flags, reinforced used flags, and then decided to analyze them. She took the tattered flags and determined how they were wearing, where the stitches began to unravel, and the kind of thread and stitches that were used to make them. Her quest to find the perfect combination of thread and stitches was successful. She figured out how to reinforce flags so that they would last longer.*

*Sister Kizzie responded to questions about volunteerism in letters to the family.*

In the course of a year I make many trips to the desert to check the purity of the water and to refill barrels. It gives me an opportunity to spend some time in the desert and to appreciate God's creation.

On water runs, we check the water to be sure it is pure and safe for drinking. We fill the tanks as needed. We check the flag to be sure it is not frayed from the wind or too faded from the sun. We check the area and pick up trash if there is any. We keep records of the amount of water

*Filling health kits*

*Checking records in the office*

143

usage at each station. Occasionally we meet migrants in need of food or medicine, which we give to them. If it is a medical emergency, we call for help.

January is a slow time until after the Feast of the Epiphany when migrants begin their journey. In another month or two we will be checking all water stations every week, and by April or May we should be given permission to set up more stations. So barrels will have to be cleaned and painted, flags sewn, and holes drilled into flagpoles.

That's about the kind of work we do mostly, along with record keeping. The hardest part is that most of the trips to the desert are in the summer when it is very hot.

I accompanied two men who have been taking food and clothing to a settlement called La Perra Flaca in southeastern Arizona and to Agua Prieta in Mexico. La Perra Flaca is located in the United States, but the conditions are as poor as those in the colonias of Agua Prieta in Mexico. These conditions prompted me to contact *We Care, We Share* in Minnesota to request that clothing be sent to Arizona. The first shipment consisted of seven tons of clothing and the second had about five tons. All were sorted and distributed in several weeks.

One day Janet helped me unload a shipment of used clothing from the Clearwater area in Minnesota. Most of this clothing would be going to Mexico. Five tons is a lot of clothing, especially when there were only seven or eight of us unloading.

The man who drove the truck from Minnesota told us that he was 250 pounds overweight at one of the weigh stations. Since he was on a charitable mission, the inspectors let him through. They probably didn't know what they would have done with 250 pounds of used clothing if they had made him empty it.

*Students from universities all over the country volunteer with Humane Borders. For example, students from Newman Center*

*A note from a St. Cloud State University student to Sister Kizzie*

at St. Cloud State University in St. Cloud, Minnesota spent several spring breaks working with Sister Kizzie.

I would be remiss if I did not write about opposition to the efforts of Humane Borders. The organization recognizes that their work is controversial and often interpreted as aiding and abetting illegal border crossers. Yes, Humane Borders says, illegal immigrants have broken the law by entering the United States without proper documentation. But, no, they should not have to pay for that decision with their lives.

In 2002, the <u>Denver Post</u> included an interview at the Organ Pipe Cactus National Monument in Arizona with John Yoakum, a long-term volunteer.

## A Reluctant Volunteer

The 300 gallons of water in the back of John Yoakum's truck make driving difficult, so he steers his rig carefully along a remote and rocky service road in this lonely preserve on the United States/Mexico border. Up ahead, through the searing heat and towering cactus, he sees a bright blue flag waving in the clear June sky. Below is a collection of turquoise plastic drums with big, reflective letters spelling out AGUA.

This day Yoakum parks the truck and proceeds, with the help

of two assistants, to unload and carry more than a dozen five-gallon jugs of water across a quarter mile of desert to replenish this station in the middle of nowhere.

"I don't want to do this. I don't think I should have to do this. I want to stop." Yoakum complains. But he says he is compelled by religious faith to act because more and more illegal immigrants are dying in these Arizona borderlands.

This year's deaths already have surpassed last year's total of 78. By contrast, only about ten died of similar causes along the entire southwest border in 1993.

So Yoakum joined Humane Borders, created to curb desert deaths and to encourage the Immigration and Naturalization Service to change its border strategy.

Beginning in early 2001, the group's members began to raise eyebrows, media attention, and the ire of anti-immigrant groups by setting up emergency water stations along popular migrant trails running north from the border.

Yoakum, a member of Tucson's First Christian Church, says he's trying to save human lives. "Jesus said the least among us are at least as important as everyone else."

*In 2004, Grupa Beta, the Mexico counterpart to the United States Border Patrol, agreed to set up water stations south of the border. Responsible for migrant safety issues, this governmental organization reported an increasing number of deaths due to dehydration. Sister Kizzie wrote to family about this huge endeavor and also her efforts to help Mexicans start small businesses.*

## Large Deployment in Mexico

I had two trips to Mexico, just along the border, this last week. Humane Borders delivered twelve water barrels with valves, stands, flags and poles, and other supplies to Reverend Mark Adams of Fronteras de Cristo in Douglas, Arizona. Together with Grupo Beta, Reverend Mark and others have found places to deploy and maintain these stations in Mexico. This is the largest deployment of Humane Borders equipment in Mexico. The stations will be located south of Cochise County in Sonora, Mexico at confidential locations.

Last year because of prolonged exposure, a record number of migrants died in Cochise County. Migrants choosing this route have to walk over dangerous, mountainous, desert terrain before they reach the border to the United States.

In Agua Prieta, across from Douglas, Arizona, we are helping families set up small businesses, such as food and secondhand clothing stores. They can sell things cheaply in their colonias but have to pay a driver to bring them food and clothes which are shipped from Minnesota to Douglas, Arizona. The store owners put 10% of their profits into a community fund. Like a cooperative, this community fund makes loans to others who want to start a business. All this is done with the hope that Mexicans will become self-sustaining citizens.

Families who do not have a wage earner or who are poorer than most others, receive vouchers from the store owners to buy food and clothing. With the vouchers, a family can have the dignity of choosing what they want to buy instead of receiving handouts. The store owners are reimbursed from the community fund for the vouchers.

## Coincidence or A Sign?

"Give us this day our daily bread. By bread alone people do not live, but by every word that comes forth from the mouth of the Lord." Deur 8:2-3

One cannot say to someone who is starving, one who has

walked the desert looking for work to feed his family: "God is Love. Pray and you will be satisfied."

Thirteen migrants, four of whom were women, walked nearly 100 miles and were tired, hungry and thirsty. They found water in water tanks. Having little money, they asked a nearby farmer for food. The farmer gave them $40 and bought food for them.

Soon after we met the migrants who asked us if we had food in our truck, and maybe socks. The students with us gave them socks. I checked my coin purse – $41. I kept $1 in case our truck broke down or we needed a phone, and gave $40 to the migrants to buy food. They said it was the $40 that the farmer had given them, which they could now give back.

Was it a coincidence that I had $41 in cash that day when I usually do not carry that much when going to the desert to check water stations? Maybe God is saying, "You are doing what you should be doing. Continue."

When He calls me, I will answer.

## Relationship with Law Enforcement

*Law enforcement on the United States/Mexico border has an impossible job. Our nation's largest law enforcement agency, the United States Border Patrol, has 80% of its agents serving this border. Their work is challenging and exceedingly dangerous with many assaults reported each year. It's an entirely different type of migrant coming across the border now than ten years ago. The huge numbers of arrests include those from countries of origin other than Mexico, Central or South America, such as Afghanistan, Iraq, and Yemen.*

*Over the last ten years, Humane Borders has earned the trust and respect of the Border Patrol agents. Although the groups have fundamental differences, neither wants people to die. The Border Patrol commends and encourages humanitarian groups,* but also warns that there will be trouble if humanitarian efforts turn into harboring illegal border crossers. The agents don't spy on water stations because they know that Humane Borders doesn't want migrants avoiding lifesaving water for fear of a trap.

*Strobe lights on the border*

Both groups work with Mexican officials and visit popular migrant meeting spots in Mexico to warn people not to illegally cross the border and not to cross the desert. Both groups distribute maps in Mexico showing locations of water stations, rescue beams, and recent deaths. The maps include the warning, *"Don't go! There's not enough water!"*

Critics say that the maps give a false sense of security to the illegal immigrants. On both sides of the border, there are public announcements warning of the desert dangers. Signs depicting blazing suns, rattlesnakes and other hazards are posted along the fence line.

During my stay in Tucson, I lived in the same residence inn as the Border Patrol and often visited with agents who were separated from family living in other parts of the country. They told me that the most rewarding part of their job was providing humanitarian assistance. Some agents are trained in search and rescue techniques, outfitted with lifesaving equipment, and are

149

*dedicated exclusively to rescuing migrants in distress.*

The Border Patrol sets up rescue beacons in various locations of the desert. Strobe lights on a thirty-foot tower are now deployed on the Tohono O'odham lands. When migrants press a button located on each tower, it alerts the Border Patrol to go to that location and pick up migrants in trouble.

Surprisingly more than half of the Border Patrol rescues are self-initiated by migrants using cell phones to call for help. The problem is there are not enough cell phone towers in the desert. We have requested that 911 emergency cell phone equipment be installed on towers which already carry cameras, radar, and other technological devices.

*To help secure the border, the Border Patrol employs Blackhawk helicopters, small helicopters, fixed-wing aircraft, drones, and other expensive high-tech equipment. They've made apprehensions in the hundreds of thousands each year. They've also confiscated hundreds of thousands of pounds of marijuana in addition to other illegal drugs, money, and weapons. These numbers are hugely significant. But billions of dollars have been spent on the United States/Mexico border during the last ten years, and still the death toll keeps climbing and the number of undocumented immigrants in the United States remains high.*

*An educational trip to the Mexico border with the leaders of Humane Borders and 25 members of a Presbyterian Church was truly an eye-opening experience for me. About 15 miles from Tucson, we stopped to fix a flat tire on one of the trucks. While waiting, we watched four Border Patrol vehicles with all their lights flashing stop a van. At least thirty occupants were taken out of the van. In one day these migrants would be back in Mexico. I heard the words 'catch and release' used often and in this very different context.*

*Attitudes in the United States regarding immigrants have turned very negative in the last few years, especially since the events of September 11, 2001. After the terrorist attack, the Border Patrol expanded surveillance and search-and-rescue efforts, added more rescue beacons, and intensified efforts at each Port of Entry. Sister Kizzie wrote the following to family.*

Security has really become tight along the border this week since the terrorist attack. It now takes about two hours just to cross the border. It usually took only a few minutes, except during rush hour when it would take about 15 or 20 minutes. Even the children coming to Douglas for school have their book bags or back packs checked. I talked to an immigration agent who said security was probably even tighter in the north.

We have had some discussions on forgiveness this week. I guess that is what we all need at a time like this. I thought I would email the president suggesting that instead of dropping bombs on other countries, we drop bundles of food. We have so many good and very generous people in the United States. This would show our good will.

*Along with the groups providing aid to the migrants, there are vigilantes and minutemen who have appointed themselves border guardians and have taken the law into their own hands. These groups are heavily armed, using high-tech equipment to round up undocumented migrants at gunpoint. In some cases, migrants have been injured and brutally killed. Sister Kizzie wrote about the vigilantes in her 2005 Christmas letter to family.*

### Militarize the Border?

Christmas, it seems, has been on television and radio for a long time. Suddenly it is almost Christmas. Exactly what happened to the time, I haven't the slightest idea.

Winter is a little easier for us because there are fewer migrants. However, the new groups of vigilantes on the border are of great concern to us. A group which started in Tombstone, Arizona wants to carry weapons and help the Border Patrol. They want to patrol our water stations. If they find immigrants, they intend to hold them at gun point until Border Patrol comes to pick them up. Their intent is to militarize the border.

We really don't want to be living in a military state. It would remind me of walking the streets in Peru and Bolivia with soldiers on each corner. If that happens, it won't be fun living this close to the border anymore. I hope someday we will have better immigration policies so the people can come to do their job and then go home as they would like to do.

My prayer for you is that many Christmas Blessings will be showered on you and that they are repeated throughout the New Year.

*Sister Kizzie wrote an article for the* <u>St. Cloud Visitor</u> *in 2006 about two different rallies she attended near Tucson. The minutemen project claims to have 15,000 volunteers patrolling the border.*

## Opposing Energies

It began on a Saturday afternoon with a kick-off rally for sending minutemen into the desert. The minutemen have taken upon themselves the duty of spotting migrant desert crossers and reporting them to the Border Patrol.

Walking up to the group already gathered on a rancher's land southwest of Tucson, I sensed energy in the air – energy clashing with the energy and feelings within my body. After listening to several speeches, the energy I sensed was filled with hate, anger, ignorance, intolerance, and racism. The anger and hate were expressed toward the desert crossers, the Border Patrol, and the federal government. The atmosphere was getting heavier and heavier. I was feeling sadder and sadder and filled with pity for those who live with such hate, anger and fear. My companions and I left at the first break. Our hearts and spirits could endure no more.

Three days later we experienced the opposite at another rally. This was an interfaith prayer rally held on the lawn of the state capitol in Phoenix. On arrival it was not hard to sense the energy filled with joy, greetings, good wishes, excitement at seeing so many willing to help our brothers and sisters. The atmosphere was filled with the presence of God. There was singing. What a joyful sound filled the air around the capitol as 1,000 or more sang!

Prayers and reflections were led by our bishop from Tucson, a rabbi, a Muslim, and the bishop of the Methodist Church. She began by saying, "God is here in our midst today."

Indeed God was. People of all faith traditions were there, praying together as one people of God.

Two different rallies. Two opposing energies filled the air.

## Desert Dangers and Deaths

*The dangers of the desert abound not only for migrants walking across, but for the volunteers as well. In her 2001 Christmas letter to family, Sister Kizzie wrote about how ill-prepared migrants are for the vastness of the desert.*

I think we are all getting too old to do this hard physical work. That's easy to say, but I haven't learned it yet. Last Thursday I wanted to jump into a dry river bed – maybe a three-foot drop. I thought I could sit, put my feet down, and drop the last foot or so.

All was fine until I squatted down to sit. I sat too hard. I thought a dagger was stabbed into my rear end. It's still a bit sensitive but almost all cleared up. The worst part was that there was nothing to show for what hurt, nor could I have shown it to anyone.

Though the world is in turmoil this year, I wish you a heart full of the peace of Jesus. Bishop Romero of El Salvador said something like this: If we live only in hope, we are living on the edge of despair. If we live with a faith-filled heart, we live with gratitude for what we have, and look forward in faith for what might be.

We are trying to set up more water stations in the desert so that maybe we can save a few lives. There were two deaths lately – that we know of. Migration was down right after the World Trade Center terrorist attack on September 11 but we know the flow will begin again right after the holidays.

*A memorial in the desert*

Last week I visited a priest in Altar, Mexico, a bit west of Nogales who is also working with migrants. We think we can work together to educate the people on the hazards of walking through the desert. Most of them just do not realize the vastness of the desert and the distances they have to walk between villages. They do not know about intense heat in the summer and cold nights in the winter. Nor are they aware of the cactus spines, which can puncture the skin and the plastic water bottles. Many lose all their water and wonder why.

The Sonoran Desert can be a deadly place. It is a haven for mesquite and greasewood trees, as well as saguaro, organ pipe and cholla cactus. Red tail hawks, elf owls and Gila woodpeckers fly its shimmering skies while snakes, badgers and coyotes forage below.

*A sign of death in the desert*

Rainfall in the Arizona portion of the Sonoran ranges from about twelve inches per year around Tucson, to three inches or less in Yuma. This spring the Tucson area experienced more than sixty consecutive days without rain. And it is hot. Stretches of days where the daytime temperature exceeds 100 degrees Fahrenheit are not unusual in Tucson.

I am trying to get the Church on both sides of the border to work together to educate the migrants. We have a start. For the first time this year we are having a joint binational Christmas Posadas, a Mexican tradition which takes place the ten days before Christmas.

*Dangers have always existed for illegal migrants. In the 1980s and early 1990s, the common causes of migrant deaths were homicides, vehicle/pedestrian accidents, and suffocation as migrants stuffed themselves into sealed boxcars and false-bottomed trucks. Drowning claimed many lives, especially when heavy rains increased the flow of rivers at the border.*

*In 2004, the Global Information Systems company, ERSI, donated mapping software to Humane Borders. Together with the Pima County Office of the Medical Examiner, they designed a cumulative map of the locations of migrant deaths, water stations, and rescue beacons. Each red dot on the map repre-sents a death. It is linked to a database which contains the name of the migrant, age, country of origin, date and cause of death, temperature on the day of death, and information about the location.*

*According to the 2009 map, there were 1,755 migrant deaths in ten years, the majority of which occurred from heat exposure or dehydration. The most frequent location of death is where a person dies after walking for two or three days north of the border. Deaths occur farther away from roads than in past years, and on the O'odham Reservation at a high rate. All one has to do is look at the death map to see that there are fewer deaths where there is water.*

*Sadly many migrants die without being identified. The bodies are turned over to the Border Patrol and then delivered to the coroner to do an autopsy and to make a list of identifying features. Records are kept in the coroner's office so that when the family in Mexico or in their home country checks up on a missing person, the coroner may be able to help with the identification process.*

In its early years, Humane Borders received just a few calls each year from families looking for missing relatives who tried to

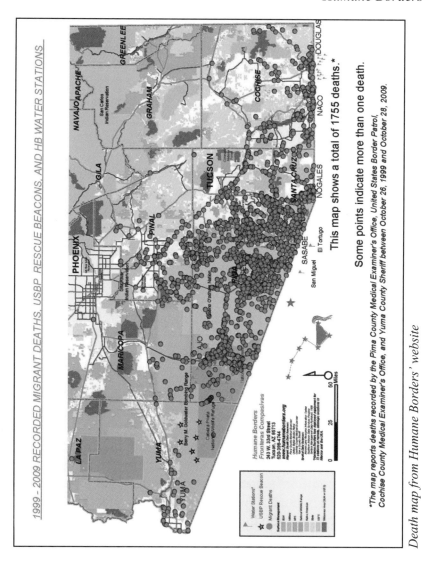

*1999 – 2009 RECORDED MIGRANT DEATHS, USBP RESCUE BEACONS, AND HB WATER STATIONS*

This map shows a total of 1755 deaths.*

Some points indicate more than one death.

*The map reports deaths recorded by the Pima County Medical Examiner's Office, United States Border Patrol, Cochise County Medical Examiner's Office, and Yuma County Sheriff between October 26, 1999 and October 28, 2009.*

*Death map from Humane Borders' website*

cross the border.  Now we have an average of two calls a week.
Over the years we've developed a network of support volunteers
to properly document missing persons.  Collaborating with other

agencies, including the Sheriff's Department, we have a valuable record-keeping system to assist in the search for missing migrants. Most families of migrants call from out of the country and don't have knowledge or the means to file a missing person's report with the appropriate agencies. We assign a bilingual volunteer to each particular missing migrant case so that the families will always have someone to talk to in the United States.

*The next letters which Sister Kizzie wrote to the family in 2002 and 2003 describe the ongoing challenges and dangers which Humane Borders and its volunteers frequently encounter on their trips to the desert.*

## Anything but Routine

The Christmas holidays have come and gone and now it is time to go back to the usual work. I'm not so sure what is usual anymore. For about a month there has been little water usage. Everyone was staying home for Christmas. Now after Epiphany they will be coming again.

One day we went to the desert to check our water stations. This part is routine, as we check regularly that the water is clean and not stale or contaminated.

Not routine that day was meeting the Border Patrol. They asked if we were being cautious. They had just found a rifle and a stash of ammunition, some for machine guns. They didn't find any people. They must have been scared away, leaving before they could pick up everything. The entire area was being patrolled. We figured these were not migrants, but drug smugglers. They're the only ones carrying arms. We assured the Border Patrol that we were being cautious.

Tomorrow I'm headed west to the Tohono O'odham Reservation to meet with the chairperson of the Baboquivari

District. They are very much afraid of the migrants and with reason. Some very bad things have happened. They might be ready now to let us help them. I'll give it a try. The chairperson said that it is like a busy freeway of human traffic going through the Reservation especially during the peak migration season.

*A hearing on the O'odham Reservation*

We now have maps of the deaths, the rescues and the water stations of the area. The death map does not look good.

*The Baboquivari District is close to Tucson. To the west of Baboquivari Peak is the Tohono O'odham Reservation. Hikers and climbers know that the mountain is of immense cultural and religious importance to the native people, and treat it with respect.*

## Not Quite Spring

St. Joseph Day! Mom's birthday! And the first day of spring is almost here. This is a good day to write a letter and wish you a Happy Easter too! I thought spring was here, but I'm still wearing three layers. It is colder inside than outside. I use a sweater inside and take it off to go out. In another month I'll wish I could take off the last layer of clothing too. In the last few weeks we have had dew points in the minus, down to -12. Not that I understand dew points very well, except that it is dry. I think a dew point lower than zero means that we can't drink water as fast as we lose it, and that is without even going to the bathroom or getting wet from sweating.

I'm still running out to the desert to fill water tanks for the migrants coming through. The priest in Altar, Mexico said that there were about 1,500 passing through their town every day, all heading through the desert west of Tucson.

Thursday evening a pickup with 41 migrants blew out a tire and rolled over. They were lying in the back stacked like cord wood. One must be pretty desperate to do that. No one was killed, but the injured overwhelmed our hospitals.

To make the hospital situation worse, another pickup with fourteen or more migrants was in an accident the next morning – sending more to the hospital. One died. We called Border Patrol and said that we would sit with the injured if they needed more help.

Several Saturdays ago I was in Ajo, about two to three hours west of Tucson. I set up a display of our work. I must have had 200 people stop by my booth. Most of the people were from environmental organizations or from the Fish and Wild Life Department. So it was great fun. This was a big event for little Ajo.

A month or six weeks ago I got orthotics put into my shoes.

*In the booth at Ajo*

Trying to adjust to these made every muscle in my body ache. I think I could have counted each muscle individually had I been so inclined. I'm still trying to decide if this is the answer. In the meantime to help the muscles, I started going to an exercise class for senior citizens. That is the hazard of being less active. It's a good thing I didn't have a desk job all my life. My muscles would have been completely atrophied. Is that spelled right? I didn't think I would ever use the word.

### Visiting Altar and Sasabe

*A group trip to Altar*

*Humane Borders makes frequent trips to the city of Altar in Sonora, Mexico. Altar, referred to as ground zero, is a meeting place for migrants from southern Mexico, Central and South America. After hearing about Altar at the Humane Borders office for two weeks, I went with a caravan of twenty volunteers, including Sister Kizzie, Sister Audrey Loher, four film makers from Notre Dame, and several photography students. Each volunteer had the same*

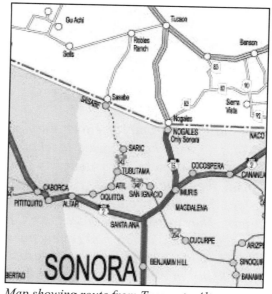

*Map showing route from Tucson to Altar*

*Barbed wire fence on the border at Sasabe*

*Border control at Sasabe*

*objective – to see and experience what is really happening across our border.*

*On the long, hot, dusty trip we crossed into Sonora, Mexico at Sasabe, where only a barbed wire fence locates the border in this part of the desert. At the Port of Entry on the Mexican side we saw many crosses reminding us of deaths in the desert.*

*From Sasabe, we drove about sixty miles on a private dirt toll road and reached Altar about midmorning. Here, we were told that every day is a festival day. Migrants come to either purchase transportation from coyotes or start the long walk to what they consider the land of opportunity. The reality is that most migrants have never been outside their village and have no knowledge of what they would do or where they would go if and when they got through the desert. They heard about places like California, New York, and Las Vegas, but very few had connections. Most could not speak English. Unfortunately migrants are told that it would take about three hours to reach Tucson which realistically is a three-day journey.*

*We walked to the town square where we saw the vans which would transport migrants from Altar to the border at Sasabe for about $15 per person. The vans typically have the seats removed and benches installed to hold as many as thirty migrants. It was easy to identify the smugglers. They strut around the plaza looking for customers, showing off their gold and silver jewelry.*

*Arranging transportation*

*Across the town square, a Mexican Red Cross trailer, paid for by the Sonoran government, serves as a medical clinic. The central plaza was busy with vendors selling food, leather goods, clothing items, amenities, trinkets and home remedies – all guaranteed to help the migrant have a safe journey. These streets*

*Packed and ready to leave*

*First aid for migrants*

163

*Catholic Cathedral in Altar*

*Main altar in the Cathedral*

*A Catholic Center to help migrants*

were lined with people, talking and shopping.

The town square is anchored by a large Catholic Cathedral. The faith of the migrants runs deep. Before they leave Altar, they attend a Mass in the Cathedral asking God to protect them and keep them safe.

Sister Kizzie and I walked a few blocks to Casa de Huespedes, a motel for migrants. On this January day the motel housed about twenty migrants. A few were resting on rugs on the bed frames, some of which were stacked four high. Others were sitting on mats or just standing around. All were nervously awaiting their journey north.

The CCAMYN, a Catholic Center for migrants, was our next stop in Altar. The Center provides food, lodging, education, counseling, and religious services. The staff gives talks about the dangers – how to recognize plants, which ones to stay away from, and which animals to be careful of in the desert. CCAMYN houses up to 40 or 50 migrants at a given time – some on their way to the United States and others on their way home.

*Grupo Beta at El Tortuga checkpoint*

On the road back to Sasabe we stopped at the El Tortuga checkpoint in the middle of the desert. We saw an orange steel structure with a roof, the only protection from the sun. Here, Grupo Beta, the Mexican counterpart to our Border Patrol, stops all vans on their way to Sasabe to check and warn migrants of the dangers and possibilities of death they will encounter if they cross the border.

*Vans lined up for checking*

*Women and children in one van*

*We saw the agents lean into vans to tell migrants to stay together, take care of women and children, watch out for snakes, scorpions, and other desert dangers.*

*We were told that the migrant count on the previous Sunday was more than 1,500 – normally not this high in January. We were at El Tortuga for less than an hour and saw hundreds of migrants. It was heart wrenching to see the large numbers of young people, some only 13 and 14 years old, and very small children held on laps. We saw only one man turn around to go back to Altar and, more than likely, back to his home. There he faces the same desperate situation he had when he left – a family to provide for and no work.*

*A throne in the middle of Sasabe?*

*... a great spot for a rest*

*Our next stop was not planned. We came upon a group of young Mexican soldiers stopping vehicles, most likely searching for drugs. Fortunately, after watching and waiting for a time, the Humane Borders' name on our trucks got us a wave through without a search.*

*We went back again through Sasabe, the border town where*

*migrants gather to cross the border into Arizona. What a contrast in this town – beautiful new modern homes with expensive cars next to low-rise clapboard and trailer homes! We arrived late afternoon to find migrants and coyotes ready to cross the border after sundown.*

*On the way back in Arizona we stopped to talk to a migrant walking alongside the road. He had been in New York without documents for six years but could no longer find work. So he was walking and hitchhiking back to Mexico. Someone had called the Border Patrol and he was waiting to be picked up.*

*The road back to Tucson was incredibly silent with each of us internally processing the experiences of the day.*

## A Busy Summer

I made a trip to the desert today to Organ Pipe Cactus National Monument to check water. We added about 35 gallons. That was actually lower than last week. It is a good thing we went there instead of the Buenos Aires Refuge because the Border Patrol and some migrants had a high speed chase on that road. We do not need to be in the middle of something like that. I guess a coyote was transporting six people from Brazil.

There have been 33 migrant deaths in the desert in just a few weeks. By putting out water, we are trying to save at least a few from dehydration. But there also are a lot of folks who don't agree with what we are doing, so some of our water tanks have been vandalized or completely stolen.

We set up a new tank on private property. The owner said migrants have been coming to his house every day asking for water. We had just put up the blue flag and were standing around talking a bit when two migrants came out from the desert. They must have been desperately thirsty because usually they would not come if we are around. We talked to them and took some pictures. Then the owner of the land took them in to give them breakfast. With us today were three reporters. I think these were free lance writers, so who knows what they will do with their photos and stories. They may let us know eventually.

The Border Patrol confirmed the dismal estimate that we had from the priest in Altar. The number of migrants entering the western half of Arizona is about 1,500 per day. Our guess is that about 80% continue north and about 20% are picked up and deported or rescued because of illness or death.

Our fires continue. Maybe our summer monsoon rains will come. So far we have had only dry thunder storms. These are not good as the lightning strikes can start more fires. A slight chance of rain is in the forecast for next week. Even slight gives us hope.

*What is life like for migrants who settle in the United States? Too often they live a nightmare. Sister Kizzie and I went to Casa Maria, a Catholic worker project for the homeless and migrants in South Tucson. An outdoor Mass was held in what was once a car port attached to the house. The Mass, said partly in Spanish and partly in English, was noisy with many people talking at the same time. There were many pigeons cooing on the roof and a dog at the altar with the priest. People gave their own petitions; some tended to go on forever – all in Spanish. Sister Kizzie said they were giving stories of their lives.*

*The attached house, called Quadalupe House, serves about 600 free meals every day.*

*Preparing for Mass at Casa Maria*

168

*The Mass was at 10:00 and already the line for lunch was very long.*

*In a letter to family, Sister Kizzie wrote about visiting a Mexican settlement east of Tucson. Unfortunately many migrants resort to living in camps in*

*Lining up for food at Quadalupe House*

*squalor. They live in dilapidated trailers or build shacks using plywood panels nailed to a wood frame and covered with plastic tarp to rainproof the rooms. Well-worn paths connect the shacks. Sewage systems are often illegal and not sanitary. Garbage is strewn around or burned in pits.*

*Few of the undocumented migrants wander far from the camps. Because of the boredom and monotony of camp life, alcoholism and prostitution are prevalent. Parties are organized for men to purchase alcohol and women brought from Mexico. Sexually transmitted diseases are common. Along with the smell of alcohol is the stench of working men living in close quarters. In the past, residents of the camp have been evicted and their shacks razed because of health concerns. But the camps have been rebuilt – again and again.*

## Life in the United States??

I visited a settlement of perhaps a hundred families about an hour or more east of Tucson. It seemed as though I was in the poorest areas of Mexico or a refugee camp. I really wanted to go there to work with them. We were making plans to do so.

But last week the county condemned their houses and sent officials to remove the people from their homes. The Border Patrol rounded them up, packed them into vans, and supposedly deported them. Apparently they are gone because they aren't answering their phones. Some have been there for twenty years. They don't have a home to go back to in Mexico.

Most of these migrants worked in the tomato greenhouses. I wondered how the company would manage after losing a lot of workers at one time. I have wanted to tour these greenhouses. I heard there are several which are ten acres in size, all under cover. I can't quite picture that in my mind.

## An Advocate for Immigration Reform

*Leading a prayer service*

*Since its beginning, Humane Borders has actively promoted public discourse on immigration issues, including social justice and reform in border, economic and environmental policies. They advocate for comprehensive immigration reform which allows migrants to work in the states and which encourages them to return home with their earnings to build a vibrant economy in their local communities and home countries.*

*Specifically their talking points call for a workable immigration policy which benefits the United States, Mexico, and Central America; a legalization process for the undocumented in the United States; a guest worker program; economic development in Mexico and other countries; a plan to demilitarize the border; and more federal aid for local medical service, law enforcement, and land owners.*

*Meeting with the media*

*Attending a civic meeting*

*An excellent speaker in English or Spanish, Sister Kizzie is often the spokesperson for Humane Borders. She takes the international phone calls, often dealing with difficult migrant situations. She is the voice of the people, traveling to churches, civic groups, and nonprofit organizations. During Humane Borders' third year in operation, Sister Kizzie kept a journal of her advocacy activities.*

As part of Humane Borders, I represented the organization at functions which promote peace, justice, and human rights. In January I spoke at a meeting with governmental officials about immigration. Or rather they came to hear our ideas of what they

*Working at a conference*

can do to ease the situation. All the organizations which work in this area were asked to speak. I was given three to five minutes. I had to either talk fast or make every word very important.

I participated in the Crop Walk and Ajo Sonoran Shindig in February, Buenos Aires Wildlife Refuge in March, St. Michael and All Angels Annual International Bazaar later in the year. I either spoke to the groups or set up tables to distribute literature and to sell items to raise money.

The Tucson Diocesan Border Ministry Committee joined with the Justice Committees of Phoenix and Hermosillo, Mexico to form the Tri-Diocesan Joint Effort. I attended the first Tri-Diocesan Conference called Encuentro 2003 which was held in Nogales, Mexico in May. Because of its success, the second is already scheduled in April 2004.

For several years I have been chaplain to women who have loved ones in prison. Their organization is called Prison Outside Arizona. Once or twice a year they have an ecumenical Kairos Retreat at which I represent the Catholic Church.

In August the actor, author, and producer of the movie The Gatekeeper visited us. The movie follows two migrants who were forced to work in a homemade methamphetamine lab in California. John Carlos Frey did five years of research to write the script for the movie. He was born in Tijuana, moved to San Diego at age three, and lived just a block or so from the border. Ever since, he has watched migrants crossing the border, getting caught and deported, or stowing away in their garages. John interviewed many of them and learned about how they were treated. He said there are hundreds of workers in California, with the owners making lots of money selling methamphetamine.

Two of the movie showings last evening were for the benefit of Humane Borders. During July we put out more than a thousand gallons of water a week. What we earned last evening will be a help.

*The March for Migrants is a yearly event held in the fall. It begins at First Christian Church and ends at Evergreen Cemetery Pauper's Graves where the unknown and unclaimed bodies are buried. The names of the identified bodies are read at the service. Desconocido, which means unknown, is said for each of the unidentified bodies. The names or the word desconocido are then placed on white crosses and carried by the marchers.*

## Not a Typical Sunday

I started the day with Mass at St. Cyril's, followed by breakfast, the Sunday newspaper, a short fifteen-minute nap, and then I was ready to go. My first stop was at the home of a friend where I will house sit for the next three days. From there I went to Humane Borders, whose offices are located in the First Christian Church, to attend the March for Migrants.

I gave the invocation at the opening prayer service. As a part of this prayer we read all the names of those who have died in the desert this year. Two of the people who had offered to read the names didn't show up. They offered because they are native Spanish speakers and could pronounce all the names correctly. Another lady and I filled in for them. Both of us have pretty good pronunciation so I guess all could understand us.

After the prayer service, I went outside until all the people lined up and started to walk. Then I went in to put things away in the chapel. I changed clothes because I didn't want to wear a T-shirt which said Humane Borders, as I was headed to the Presbyterian Church for a memorial service for a lady who had worked with refugees, farm laborers, and the poor since the 1970s. What a beautiful service it was. Amy was loved by everyone, probably because she always had time for everyone. During the sanctuary days there must have been 10,000 refugees who passed through this church. I think Amy spoke to every one of them. After the sanctuary days, she stayed at the church and started educational programs and a clinic for the migrants. All her programs are still going strong.

What a Sunday it was. I was at the Catholic Church in the morning, the First Christian Church in the afternoon, and the Presbyterian Church in the evening.

Thank God all Sundays aren't like this.

*Sister Kizzie wrote the following opening prayer and reflection which were reprinted in the November - December 2002 issue of the BorderLinks publication of Loaves & Fishes.*

## March for Migrants Prayer

Together we pray, bringing our thoughts, our feelings, our concerns to our God.

Loving God, Creator of all. Today, You gathered together a group of people who are very concerned about our brothers and sisters who are suffering. Thank You for accompanying us on our march, for leading and guiding us, for inspiring us to do what sometimes can be dangerous and scary. At those times, whisper into our hearts and ears what we may have forgotten. Remind us that You are the strength inside us, the courage that gives us hope and helps us act when action is needed.

Your whisperings remind us that people have been migrating from the very beginning. If indeed there was one Adam and one Eve, their descendants migrated, always looking for a place where there was sufficient food, or where life could be better. The same was true for most of our ancestors.

We were those migrants and now we say that we belong here. This land is ours and it can't hold more people.

Lord, You have given us minds to seek knowledge. You have led minds to develop DNA testing and many other ways to understand the paths of migration.

You Yourself, Lord, were a migrant. You fled because You had a mission to accomplish. You didn't know what it was at the time but eventually it became clear. When things are not clear to us, give us the hope that what we are doing will lead to good. Your mission which became clear after You grew older must not have been easy, for You turned many things upside down. You did what those in authority did not like to see. You had the courage to do it anyway, without considering the consequences.

You called those who are poor, Blessed. You called those who mourn, Blessed. You called those who are humble, Blessed.

I am not sure that I fit into these categories. There are a lot of people here with me today. I don't know if they fit into these categories. They will have to decide that for themselves. If we're not sure whether we are poor, or we mourn, or are humble, then I suppose we aren't. So can we not be called Blessed?

That puts us in a dilemma, and again You give us an answer. You said, "I was hungry and you fed me; thirsty and you gave me to drink; a stranger and you took me in."

Are you telling me that here in this dry desert of Arizona where temperatures dehydrate us in a very short time, and where water is not plentiful, in fact often very scarce especially when we have a drought, that You want us to give water to everyone who is thirsty? Even if we don't know them? Even if they are

*Giving the opening prayer*

*Marching out of the church*

*Placing the crosses*

foreigners?

We all know the story of Moses crossing the desert to save Your people. You helped him find water to save them from dehydration. None of us have hit a rock to bring a stream of water in the desert, but You have provided us with an inspiration to carry water there.

A year ago was the September 11 attack. We asked, "How could this happen to us? How could anyone commit such an act of terrorism against us and kill so many of our countrymen?"

Today we also ask, "How can we allow our brothers and sisters in other parts of the world to go hungry? To receive such little pay that if they buy food, they cannot buy anything else? And if they buy something else, they cannot buy food?

Lord, have I helped?  Have we all helped?  Has our country helped this situation?"

We ask.  We try to understand.  We try to help.  Blessed are those of good will who are willing to help.

Lord, where You are, there is hope.  Any situation can change for the better, especially where people have the courage to speak the truth and damn the consequences.  You gave us a good example.  Following your example should be easy, but it takes so much courage to speak the truth, and often a lot more courage to damn the consequences.  My prayer these days is that You fill everybody with strength, every heart with courage, and every mind with inspiration to say, "Here I am, Lord.  Send me to be Your hands and Your love to our brothers and sisters."  Amen

*In 2007, there were 246 crosses.  In 2008, after the names of 175 deaths and an equal number of unnamed deaths were read, the March for Migrants went to the Federal Courthouse.  The speeches focused on the need for church leaders, state and local governmental officials, O'odham leaders, and humanitarian groups to do more to end migrant deaths.  In 2009 there were more than 200 white crosses; 101 were unnamed deaths.*

## Letter to the Mexican Governors

*Sister Kizzie's advocacy extended beyond local events and speaking engagements.  For example, she wrote the following letter (translated into English) to the Mexican governors encouraging them to help their people.*

January 10, 2003

My name is Sister Elizabeth Ohmann.  I am a part of Humane Borders which has been in operation for more than two years.

One of our concerns is to save the lives of our brothers and sisters who are coming across the border into the United States to earn a living and to support their families. For almost two years we have been placing water in the desert to save the migrants from dehydration. We feel that we have a moral obligation to save people from dying if we are able to do so.

Many migrants who come across the border are not very well informed about temperatures, distances, and dangers in the desert. It would be better for them to receive this information before they leave their homes. They could make a better decision as to whether they should leave home or remain in Mexico – whether they want to risk their lives or not!

I believe it is important or maybe even morally obligatory for the government to inform the people of dangers that threaten their lives. So I suggest that a program be initiated to educate the people about the geography of the land which they are planning to cross. This could be done in their home areas before they leave. It could be done in the areas where the migrants gather the day before they cross the border. Consider Altar, for example. We have contact with Padre Rene Castaneda and the community center which feeds and houses the migrants. We have given them maps of the most dangerous areas and maps of where they can find water.

We consider the most dangerous areas to be where the most deaths have occurred and the highest concentration of deaths was immediately west of the Baboquivari Mountains. We have not been given permission to place water in that area. Therefore it would be safer for the migrants to stay away from there and travel in safer areas.

It is important that the migrants know the topography of the area and that they know landmarks. We are most willing to cooperate with you by providing maps to those who like Padre Rene are preparing the migrants.

Many times I hear migrants say they were not aware of the vastness of the desert and of the great distances they had to walk or how many days it would take them. The smugglers often give wrong information. It is up to others, like you, to give correct information.

Thank you very much for your time.

Sister Elizabeth Ohmann, OSF *(Signed)*

*One of the most prestigious events at which Sister Kizzie was invited to speak was the conference on the United States/Mexico border hosted by the Universidad Autonoma de Baja California in Mexicali in March 2004. The Mexican University had invited organizations and individuals who work with human rights and immigration issues.*

*The conference coincided with the opening of an exhibit on the border in the University's Cultural Studies Museum. This exhibit has a reconstructed desert camp and a simulated detention experience where visitors are transferred into border crossers confronted with a twelve-foot replica of the border wall. The exhibit includes a Humane Borders water station, a death map, and numerous artifacts.*

## Universidad Autonoma de Baja California in Mexicali

Thank you very much for inviting Humane Borders to be present here with you this evening. My name is Elizabeth Ohmann. I am a Franciscan Sister from Little Falls, Minnesota. For almost twenty-five years I have been living in Arizona and acquainting myself with the border and border issues.

This evening I am representing Humane Borders. Humane Borders was founded June 11, 2000 to respond in a humanitarian way to the people risking their lives crossing the United

States/Mexico border and to advocate for changes in United States policies that perpetuate this risk

How do we, as Christians, as people who call everyone our brothers and sisters, and are called upon to love our neighbors, respond to the deaths that are taking place in the desert in our state or as I call it, in our backyard?

Since the beginning of Humane Borders, we have accomplished much in providing humanitarian assistance and advocating for policy change by carving out a social space in which persons of conviction can and will provide meaningful assistance to persons in peril, at the same time working within the confines and constraints of our legal-political system.

The politics of migration are neither liberal nor conservative. We continue to have an emergency situation. We have a matter of life and death that must be addressed by the federal, state and tribal governments, as well as all individuals in the United States and in Mexico.

United States/Mexico border policies are fatally flawed.

*Sister Kizzie on center stage at Universidad Autonoma de Baja California*

Migrants are dying in record numbers in our deserts, in the canals of California, in the Rio Grande and on our roads. Just in southern Arizona the deaths have increased dramatically in the last few years. In 1998 only eleven deaths were recorded. In 1999 there were 29. In 2000, 44 deaths. In 2001, 78 deaths. In 2002, 163 deaths and in 2003, 205.

This outrageous increase is somewhat due to record keeping. Good records were not kept for those first few years. Until last year we received this statistical information only from Border Patrol. Last year, The Arizona Republic newspaper of Phoenix compiled a list by name and location of the known deaths gathered from Border Patrol, the Mexican Consulates, and county coroners. That accounts for the dramatic increase to 205. These are the known deaths. After this list was completed, five skeletons were found west of Tucson. No one knows if there are more.

The Southwest Strategy of the Immigration and Naturalization Service which includes closing down the urban areas of the border with more personnel, fences, and technology has a certain, local logic to it in terms of crime reduction, but it also has tragic consequences. United States Border Patrol inaugurated Operation Gatekeeper, Safeguard, Hold the Line and a few others in the urban areas. Increasing the security and closing the urban areas feed the coyote or human smuggling industry and force the migrants to the remote desert areas.

Migrants jump fences in the most fortified areas and require expensive, non-reimbursed medical services. Migrants cross deserts that are both dangerous and environmentally delicate. Migrants trespass on private land causing distress to the landowners while breaking down fences allowing animals to escape. The sheer numbers walking across the grazing land and deserts trample down the delicate vegetation, which already is stressed due to the drought. All this while the Mexican baby-boomers are working for the United States baby-boomers, dramatically fueling the economy and the United States tax coffers.

The concern of landowners also brings up the concern of vigilantism. Vigilantism mirrors United States border policies in general. It is embedded in the police powers of the general public and in the rights of individuals to bare arms.

There are several vigilante groups in southeastern Arizona, particularly in Cochise County. The most visible is Ranch Rescue located in Texas and Arizona. They seem to be most concerned with private property laws and national sovereignty questions. They are limited to working on private property and pay their own expenses.

Another group, the Civil Homeland Defense, is run by Chris Simcox. He and his followers operate on private property and on some State Trust Lands. They are limited as to where they can legally operate. The third group, American Border Patrol, are neither limited by geographical areas nor by finances. They have very sophisticated instruments for tracking migrants in the desert. These groups favor militarization of the border.

Humane Borders does not believe that militarization of the border is in our best interest. Can the United States shut down the border? No. Those studying the politics of immigration will conclude that the United States has neither the political will nor the financial resources to do a complete interdiction of migrants at the border. To those who suggest it can, I wonder if they have considered the cost to taxpayers and to the economy.

South to north migration is an inexorable flow of humanity toward a better life. Employer sanctions have been stopped because of our insatiable appetite for cheap labor and the contributions to the American economy.

It is not the migrants who cross the border looking for work to feed themselves or their families that concern me and many others the most. It is the drug dealers. They often come armed and dangerous and have little respect for life. They use innocent people to carry the drugs across the border and to show them the way through the desert. Particularly on the Tohono O'odham Tribal lands, they will use the local people, often children or youth, to carry the burdens. They pay them with drugs, leading to further drug abuse and gangs and criminal violence.

Some measures are being taken and some efforts are being made to control, if not solve, the migration issue. Numerous efforts to draft guest worker legislation are underway across the nation as attention turns both to national security and economic interests.

President George W. Bush proposed a new temporary worker program. He recognized that the United States was built and developed by migrants and children of migrants. As a Texan who lived close to the border, he has known many immigrant families, mainly from Mexico. He said they have brought with them values of faith in God, love of family, hard work and self-reliance. These are the very values on which the United States was built. As a nation which values immigration, and depends on immigration, we should have immigration laws that work and make us proud. We do not. And many of us are not proud of that.

President Bush's new immigration proposal is a temporary program that will match willing foreign workers with willing American employers. The workers' legal status will last three years and be renewable for another three years. It will have an end. Undocumented workers, already in the United States will be required to pay a one-time fee to register. Those applying from abroad will pay no fee. Workers will be expected to return home after their work time has expired.

President Bush is hoping to work with the foreign countries so that there is a financial incentive to the workers for returning home, such as giving the temporary workers credit for the time they worked in the United States and putting a portion of their earnings into a saving account which can be collected on their return home.

Those wishing to remain in the United States after their six years of work may apply for citizenship in the usual way. This proposal of the president has not yet been written up as a bill nor presented to Congress. Therefore, there is no formal discussion on it as yet.

In the meantime, many concerned citizens and activists are discussing the contents and the possible good effects as well as the limitations of the proposal. Some believe that the proposal is too limited. It actually presents more questions than it does answers. These questions are being discussed by our political leaders. There is no plan that those workers returning home after three or six years will be guaranteed a job there. The integrity of the family is not mentioned. Will the worker be in the United States alone and the family in Mexico with only infrequent visits? For those choosing citizenship in the United States after the years of work, will that include the rest of the family or will this worker proposal break up the family?

In the temporary worker program, President Bush says he is aware of the family values that the Mexicans have. Are there provisions for participation by the undocumented already living in the United States?

Labor activists are concerned that the workers will have no rights. That they will be tied to the one employer and have no recourse if conditions are not good. Will worker dignity be upheld? Will workers be able to organize or will unions be able to organize workers? Will the needs of our neighbor, Mexico, be taken into consideration when quotas are set for work visas?

These are some of the many questions that we as faith-based communities are asking because we are nonmarket, nongovernmental organizations. Business and politics have their own interests to protect. The questions of the faith communities are important because they have been the single largest source of support for the foreign-born before the United States was founded and they continue to be so. Faith-based organizations or communities are more person oriented. Each person is our brother and sister.

There are several other bills being proposed. None are moving along very quickly and I don't think they will this year as it is an election year. This happens every time there is an election, whether it is in a country, an organization, a church, or wherever. Things are at a standstill until after the election.

Mexico is not without responsibility to the migrants. Grupo Beta warns migrants of the dangers of crossing the desert, but a far more extensive program of education needs to be in place. We gave them maps of where water stations could be found, but we are no longer permitted to do so. When I meet migrants one or two kilometers north of the border, they ask me, "How much farther is it to Oregon?"

It is heart breaking. It also tears my heart when I see children in the desert or hear that the migrants have been told that they can walk to Phoenix or Los Angeles or Las Vegas in just a few hours.

Humane Borders supports legal status to undocumented persons living and working in the United States. Security concerns demand that we know who is here. The matricula consular is actually a step in that direction. Humane Borders supports legalized work opportunities for migrants wanting to work in the United States. If legalized, the workers would be able to enter at a Port of Entry and would not have to take the dangerous walk through the desert. We support updating the Immigration and Naturalization Service registry and exempting Mexico from the worldwide quota of visas. These initiatives would reduce the number of deaths in the desert.

We are dedicated to taking death out of migration.

## Future of Humane Borders

*The year 2010 was a transitional year for Humane Borders. Among the changes were renewed leadership, more decision making and responsibility given to the Board of Directors, and a new location with a secure parking lot. The organization obtained charitable status as a 501(c)(3) organization. As such, it can directly accept tax-deductible gifts and contracts to support its work. Today Humane Borders works with more than sixty affiliated organizations including congregations, human rights groups, denominational agencies, universities, legal assistance organizations, and governmental agencies.*

*The Spring 2010 Humane Borders Newsletter included a summary of recent activities.*

This year since January, Humane Borders has hosted and facilitated educational experiences for groups and individuals from all around the world. More than 150 volunteers participated with Humane Borders and were able to observe our operations and learn more about the border and the complexities of border policy. Students from Colorado State University, University of Michigan, University of Kansas, Stanford University and Edgewood College participated in activities with Humane Borders staff and volunteers. With their help we were able to pick up more than 3,000 pounds of trash throughout southern Arizona and generate more than $3,000 in donations and mission support fees.

*Early in 2010 Humane Borders decided to look for a more secure place to store their trucks and equipment. Over the years they had vandalism and theft in the parking lot at First Christian Church. A truck had been stolen and later recovered on the east side of Tucson. It had been used to steal construction materials from building sites. Another truck was stolen and later recovered* in Douglas. It had been used to transport drugs across the border. In 2008 the tires were slashed on all the trucks in the parking lot. In 2009 trucks parked at the church were vandalized on several occasions.

Humane Borders moved to its new location at the House of Neighborly Service in South Tucson in 2010. The staff and volunteers are thankful for the affordable office space and secured parking area.

After ten years the organization's humanitarian challenge is still to provide water in the desert. Setting up a station is complicated. It involves coordinating the agreement of a land-owner, documents, inspections, insurance, vehicles, pumps, equipment, satellite phones, and medical supplies. The Tohono O'odham Nation has not yet given permission to install water stations. Unofficially water stations have been set up, but officials continue to confiscate the equipment. In the June 2011 Humane Borders Newsletter, Board President Felipe Lundin announced a new dialogue with the O'odham Nation. Last year 67% of the migrant deaths occurred on the Reservation.

Humane Borders continues to devote considerable resources to telling the story of the plight of the migrant in local, regional, national and international media. The archive contains more than 2,500 printed articles about Humane Borders and the volunteers. Articles come from more than 400 news agencies including Russian, Mandarin Chinese, Pakistani, Pacific Rim, and all over Europe and Spanish-speaking nations.

Today there are more than 250 videos plus several documentaries featuring Humane Borders. For example, <u>Crossing Arizona</u>, created by Dan Devivo and Joseph Mathew, features Mike Wilson from Humane Borders and his efforts to place water along the most deadly migrant Baboquivari Trail on the Tohono O'odham Reservation. <u>Dying to Live</u> was produced at Notre Dame. Rachel Antel's <u>Death on a Friendly Border</u> tells *the story of Yolanda Gonzales Garcia's death in Arizona and her family living in Mexico.*

*In June 2011, Humane Borders celebrated its ten-year anniversary. How is success measured?*

When Humane Borders was founded, no one ever dreamed that we would still be in business today. Between 1994 and 2009, more than 5,000 migrants died in the deserts that span the United States border with Mexico. Nearly 1,900 of these died in Arizona. Undoubtedly there would have been more deaths without Humane Border's water stations strategically placed in the desert.

*In 2011 two leaders of Humane Borders, Board President, Felipe Lundin, and Executive Director, Sofia Gomez, wrote the following testimonial giving Sister Kizzie credit for its success.*

Sister Elizabeth, a founding and current Board member of Humane Borders, was not only instrumental but also key in the agency's development and mission. Sister Elizabeth was present at the onset of Humane Borders and is the longest serving member of the Board.

Through the years Sister Elizabeth has served on numerous water trips, fund raisers, educational presentations, and delegation visits. Her calm yet strong leadership during the years has been essential especially in trying times. Never self promoting, she is always ready to roll up her sleeves and lend a hand.

Sister Elizabeth is a person of humility, a knowledgeable individual who brings a wealth of experience to Humane Borders. She is quiet in nature but when she speaks, she makes a lot of sense. Her previous experience at BorderLinks and missions in Latin America as an educator, administrator and pastoral care provider in the Native American community in southern Arizona provides Humane Borders with a strong foundation.

Sister Elizabeth devoted not only her time and expertise but when Humane Borders encountered financial struggles, she financially supported the cause. This was particularly crucial during Humane Borders recent transition. Without her assistance, Humane Borders may not have survived this past year. She has done this selflessly.

Sister Elizabeth's life of service and commitment to social justice and humanitarian work has inspired many and will continue to do so for a long time. That is her legacy.

We are very fortunate to be blessed by her presence and service. Thank you, Sister Elizabeth. We are immensely indebted to you!

Felipe Lundin and Sofia Gomez *(Signed)*

## Way of the Cross for the Migrants

*During the summer of 2011, Sister Kizzie returned to live at the Franciscan Convent in Little Falls, Minnesota. Her passion for the less fortunate is reflected in the Way of the Cross which she wrote for the migrants.*

1.  Jesus is condemned to death.
    Migrants are condemned to a death walk through the desert.
2.  Jesus takes up His cross.
    A mother carries her child through the desert to save themselves from starvation.
3.  Jesus falls the first time.
    Migrants are picked up and deported.
4.  Jesus meets His mother.
    A volunteer looks into the eyes of a dehydrated, starving migrant.

5. Simon of Cyrene helps Jesus carry His cross.
   One carries his brother to safety.
6. Veronica wipes the face of Jesus.
   Volunteers give care packages to migrants.
7. Jesus falls the second time.
   The sick and injured crawl to safety.
8. Jesus meets the women of Jerusalem.
   Migrants meet a rescue team saying "Please notify our families."
9. Jesus falls the third time.
   Smugglers abandon the fallen and sick migrants.
10. Jesus is stripped of His garments.
    The suffering are stripped of their dignity.
11. Jesus is nailed to the cross.
    Cactus spines stab the bodies of migrants.
12. Jesus dies on the cross.
    A migrant dies alone in the desert.
13. Jesus is taken down from the cross.
    Rescuers pick up dead bodies.
14. Jesus is laid in the tomb.
    Unidentified bodies are buried in an unknown country by an unknown people.
15. Jesus rises from the dead.
    There are no longer foreigners. All are united in Christ.

# Part Four
# A Teacher at Heart

*Does it take a child, who in our eyes is not gifted
with understanding the meaning of the written word,
and who has no ability to learn facts,
to teach us the meaning of the love of Jesus,
and what is important and what isn't?*

Sister Kizzie, 1960

*These are stories of Sister Kizzie's years as an educator. The first part includes stories of her teaching experiences in the elementary schools of the St. Cloud Diocese in central Minnesota. The most gratifying years were those spent with special-needs students. The next part is about tutoring her grandniece, Jennie, who suffered a massive head injury when she was struck by a truck while riding her bicycle. The last stories are from Ndoleleji, Tanzania and Yarnell, Arizona.*

## Elementary Schools in Minnesota

*From 1954 to 1967, Sister Kizzie taught in several elementary schools of the St. Cloud Diocese in central Minnesota. She received her first assignment at St. Joseph's School in Waite Park after only one year of college.*

Until 1954, St. Joseph's School in Waite Park only had grades five through eight. In the fall of 1954, a new section was built on the school and the first four grades were added. Due to a shortage of teachers that year, many of the nuns began to teach – after only one year of college. We were as new as the new part of the

191

school.

In my second year, I was asked if I would take one half of the third grade to a classroom in the old part of the school. This classroom was right off the gym. On the first day, my students, individually selected by the principal, and I went to our classroom. Because there was a shortage of desks, we only had a few tables and folding chairs. We borrowed desks from the public school and would have them within the first week.

These inconveniences became a source of motivation for good behavior. Since we had no desks, it would be harder to study, so every day we would do some type of craft. There was an *if* clause attached, and the students would have to agree to it. During crafts, we could talk, but not so loud that we could be heard in the new part of the school. The first week was fun. Then the desks arrived and we became a regular classroom.

We were still special as we were the only ones right by the gym. Occasionally we used it.

*Next Sister Kizzie taught third grade at Our Lady of Victory School, a new parochial school in Fergus Falls. In 1957, she was transferred to Alexandria to teach third and fourth grades in the new St. Mary's School. Five years later, St. John's in Foley began a new school and she was transferred again. There Sister Kizzie was assistant principal and taught second grade.*

## Too Much Help

Daily Mass was part of the school day's routine. Finding the perfect time of the day for Mass seemed to be the biggest problem. When fasting before receiving Holy Communion was changed to one hour, Mass could be celebrated at any time of the day. The least disruptive time to the teaching schedule was to have Mass immediately before the noon lunch. Thus, it was.

It appeared to me that many children were getting sick or feeling faint during Mass. I was sure it was because they were hungry. After all, it was nearly lunch time.

One day Sister Winifred, who often came from the hospital to attend Mass, noted, "Most of them are from your class. What do you do when you go out with them?"

That was easily explained. "They are weak because they are hungry, so I give them a cracker or a cookie." Most reasonable, I thought.

In all her wisdom, Sister Winifred said, "Maybe if you weren't so good to them, they wouldn't get sick so often."

How right she was.

## Knowing Jesus

Mary, with a face as beautiful as that of an angel, found it very difficult to learn certain things. Orally, Mary could read with more clarity and expression than any gifted third grader. But Mary could not comprehend the meaning of the words. Why she could read orally with expression but with no comprehension was a secret known to God and Mary. As Mary's teacher I marveled and wondered.

Mary seemed to have other secrets with God. As she received Holy Communion one morning at our daily Mass, the host slipped out of her mouth and fell to the floor. Perhaps the host accidentally bumped her teeth and flipped out, or as Mary explained, "I just didn't get my mouth closed on time."

This was the time when Communion was received on the tongue. No one but a priest was to touch the host. Nor was the host to touch the teeth or the roof of the mouth. There were so many details to remember.

Mary remained unflustered. Jesus fell. Mary bent over, picked up Jesus, took the host, and ate it. Mary and Jesus were fine. It was not so for the rest of the students. They gasped, lost all church etiquette and decorum, and literally ran back to me in the pew to report that Mary had touched the host. I told the children to kneel down and we would talk about it later in school.

All the commotion had Mary in tears. I put my arms around her and asked what happened. She looked up to me with all the innocence of one in love with Jesus and said, "Jesus fell down and I had to pick Him up."

Does it take a child, who in our eyes is not gifted with understanding the meaning of the written word and who has no ability to learn facts, to teach us the meaning of the love of Jesus and what is important and what isn't?

Out of the mouth of babes.

## Teaching Children with Special Needs

*The years which Sister Kizzie spent teaching special-needs students were especially gratifying. From 1960 to 1963, she taught in a combination room with students from grades four through six who found learning difficult. Some were certainly slow learners, but she knew some were bright but unable to learn in the conventional sense. By the time she got them in her class, most of them hated school so that they no longer could learn.*

*As you read these stories about Sister Kizzie, you will understand her love for the special-needs children, especially their simple life style, and their easy laughter.*

## Balancing Birds

On coping with learning disabilities, I have had to do some of that myself. I am somewhat dyslexic so I reverse numbers, letters in words, and rarely get left and right correct. But one can learn to deal with it mostly through a lot of concentration.

I loved the school-challenged and the learning-challenged students. These were probably the best years of my teaching. Most of these students didn't like school because it was so hard. So my first objective was to help them develop a liking for going to school and a love for studying. During the first week of school we only did fun things, such as crafts, stories, and talking about good things. One craft project was paper folding. The most important lesson was to follow directions. In the end we each had a bird in the hand. We tied the birds to the ends of dowels and hung them in such a way that they balanced. We were the envy of all the students in the school. We had *balancing birds*.

We organized a mission group, with officers and all. One boy, newly elected president, couldn't wait to get home to tell his mother, "Never in my whole life did I think I would be a president."

That evening his mother called to tell me how happy she was to know her son liked to go to school.

*At that time, there was so little known about how to teach special-needs students. Sister Kizzie seemed to have a natural insight to do whatever it took to have some degree of success. She tried all the tricks she knew, spending a great deal of time with each student individually.*

*There were usually about 18 children in the special-needs class which she taught for the three years that the program existed. Several of the parents told her it was the first time their child looked forward to going to school.*

## Facts! Facts! Facts!

Facts can be so incomprehensible – entirely impossible for some, while easy for others. Students with difficulties learning, understanding, and remembering, often try the patience of teachers. At the same time they can also be the source of great joy.

After having taught, explained, and repeated at least 200 times that $2 + 2 = 4$, I wondered whether there was yet another way to say the same. There must be, though I did not know the clarifying moment nor the exact day it would actually happen.

But one day, revelation! Jerry jumped up from his desk with the greatest of announcements. "You know what, Sister, when we put these two and these two together, we get four all together. $2 + 2 = 4$."

"That's wonderful! Look what Jerry figured out!"

The children laughed and applauded. I'm sure there was greater joy in our classroom than there was in the science lab when a vaccine was discovered or a new species was identified.

*Nearly fifty years later, one of her former special-needs students met someone who worked for the Franciscan Sisters. He asked her if she knew Sister Elizabeth, his teacher for three years in the special class. She had made a huge impression on his life. Since it is policy not to give out names and addresses without permission, his name and address were sent to Sister Kizzie who then contacted him.*

June 2006

Dear Sister Elizabeth Ohmann,

Thank you for writing and for the beautiful card. Life has been quite wonderful for me. After leaving St. Mary's, the public school system put me in speech therapy and remedial reading. I became and continue to be an avid reader. While high school was filled with the usual traumas, in college I really began to realize the wonders of the world. One of my professors became a bit fascinated with my brain and put me through hundreds of tests. He was awestruck by the results. I scored in the top one-millionth on some, often presenting the highest score ever recorded. In others I would plummet to the bottom 18 to 30%. He helped me discover how my mind worked and I helped him understand the departmentalizing functions of the brain.

In college, I met some magnificent scholars, authors, college presidents, and professors from St. John's, St. Cloud, and many other universities. I fondly remember discussing philosophy, social issues, religion, and history for hours with them. I was awestruck that these men were sometimes fifty or even sixty years my senior; yet we shared our thoughts in an egalitarian atmosphere. At this time, I developed my personal beliefs.

Life then took me to the Dominican Republic where I lived in the mountains north of Santo Domingo. I worked at a school that became the first American-accredited bilingual school. At the same time, I became involved with a group feeding the children at the local hospital. We had to feed the children ourselves. If we just left the food, it would get stolen and the children continued to be hungry. We tried to get some of the children adopted in the United States, but the bureaucracy was impossible. There was a total unwillingness of institutions to help outside the system. So, after getting the children healthy, some had to go back to where they came from, and died. Eventually we formed an organization to provide care independent of the corrupt system.

We returned to the United States and settled in the Appalachian region of southern Ohio. There my wife and I opened a childcare center in which our daughter was the first student. We soon had two more daughters and two more centers providing care for 175 children from newborn to school age. Then we added summer camps and after-school programs.

The Ohio State University was amazed at the success we had with our children. More than 90% of these children who were typically considered below average were now testing as gifted. We had children with Down Syndrome who made amazing gains both mentally and physically. The governor appointed me to the Ohio Daycare Advisory Board. There I found a lot of typical bureaucrats unable or unwilling to understand the elements of success. While I did serve two terms, again I was disappointed in how self-important and uncaring institutions can be.

While I still suffer from my learning disabilities and have to look at my driver's license to correctly write my address and need to look at my business card for my phone numbers, I have developed a lot of coping mechanisms. As I have progressed through life, I have always been grateful that at St. Mary's I learned three important proficiencies. The first is the importance of speech and the use of complete and correct sentence structure whenever one speaks. Second is the importance of middle class manners and mannerisms. And the third is the importance of clear and concise ethics without regard for the consequences.

While the first two have permitted me to conceal my learning disabilities, the third has served me best of all. I have an amazing community of friends that supports and sustains me. I could not have asked for a better life. I will always be thankful that these skills were learned at St. Mary's School.

Clyde *(Signed)*

*Unfortunately the special classroom was closed after three years. Fortunately Sister Kizzie could now complete her college degree.*

I had the year to study instead of teaching. When I started teaching in the 1950s, the Catholic schools were so short of teachers. It was only after I finished one year of college that I, along with my classmates, was asked to begin teaching. We could complete our college degree by attending summer school.

Each spring we were given a white letter telling us where we would teach the next year and which grade we'd have. I had been teaching a few years when one spring all the white letters arrived and I had none. Everyone in the house wondered what had happened. Was I not to teach anymore? Was I leaving the convent? What was the reason?

I had no answer. I didn't expect to be put out into the street. The next day a call came saying my name was missed because the special classroom I had was to be closed. Since teachers were assigned to all the other classes, I was free and could return to St. Catherine's to finish my degree. By the end of the year, I only needed six more credits in a foreign language. Georgetown was the only place which taught a six-credit summer course in Spanish II. By the end of the summer I graduated from St. Catherine's.

*Sister Kizzie was teaching at St. Mary's School in Alexandria when she was selected to do mission work in Peru. The fourth graders composed a song entitled 'All Through the Year' for her farewell program. With the money raised during Lent, the students at St. Mary's purchased a washing machine*

*Sister Kizzie with Anita, Renee and Thomas at St. Mary's School in Alexandria, Minnesota*

---

**All Through the Year**

You must go and we will miss you
All through the year.
We will ask the Lord to bless you
All through the year.
Thank you for the things you taught us,
For the joy and cheer you brought us.
May the Holy Spirit guide you
All through the year.

---

*for $100 for the sisters in Zepita, Peru and contributed the remaining $16 to help pay for Sister Kizzie's airplane ticket to Puerto Rico. Her students were not eager to see her leave, but all wished her well in her future mission work on the Altiplano in Peru. Sister Kizzie left in August 1967 to study Spanish for three months in Puerto Rico.*

## Many Beginnings

Each year I was privileged to have a week or more in retreat. It is a time to pray, meditate, and be alone with God. It is a time to reflect on what has been and what is to come. Thinking back over the years, it seemed to me that I was constantly beginning new schools, new organizations, and new living situations. Sometimes it was reorganizing the work or reorganizing structures in my life.

Teaching in my first elementary school without much preparation was itself an adjustment. Beginning in the Waite Park school with newly-expanded primary grades was a double adjustment. The second year of teaching, I was asked if I would take all the problem students, which meant the most troubled learners, and the five or six very good students in third grade. What a challenge! But it turned out to be a very good year.

The third year of teaching was a move to Fergus Falls to open a new school. The fourth year was to open another new school in Alexandria. This time I stayed for five years. The following fall, Foley opened a new school. I was there to begin again. Each move meant teaching in a new environment, living with different sisters, and becoming acquainted with new people.

Three years later brought a new beginning, but it was not teaching in a school. It was to live in a different country – Peru, learn a new language, live among a new people, and live an entirely different life style than the one I knew so well.

Returning to the states, Breck School in Minneapolis invited me to join their faculty. Breck School is an Episcopal-affiliated school. I was the first Catholic sister to teach there. Teaching again after ten years was an adjustment, as was teaching in a very elite school where children had to pass an entrance exam to be admitted.

During the first week, I prepared lesson plans as I had done

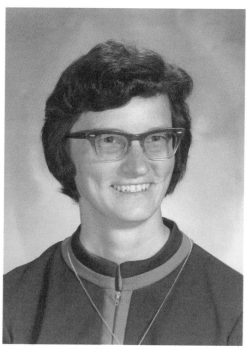

*Teaching at Breck School in Minneapolis*

201

years ago. I had not taken into consideration that during the last three years before going to Peru, I taught children with learning difficulties. Now in front of me, I had a class of above-average children, all eager to learn. My entire week's lesson plans were spent in one morning!

What an adjustment! Not only had ten years passed, but life in the United States had changed and teaching had changed as well. After two years, a warmer climate seemed to be calling. St. Cyril's School in Tucson, Arizona planned to add a Spanish program to their curriculum the following year. I offered to develop the program, locate materials, and teach for two years. After that, I believe a native person should teach the language.

Shoveling snow to get the car out of the garage helped me make the decision to move to Tucson. Another new beginning!

## Tutoring Jennie

*On a Friday afternoon in 2003, Sister Kizzie's grandniece Jennie was hit by a truck on a Tucson street while riding her bicycle home from school. With Sister's tutoring, she was able to return to her classes. Jennie has two siblings, Emily and Michael, mother, Amy, and grandparents, Janet and Dr. John Haas. Janet is Sister Kizzie's sister.*

### Jennie's Miracle
Janet Haas

Sister Kizzie's abundant teaching skills were put to good use in the family when tragedy struck in the fall of 2003. Her eleven-year-old grandniece, Jennie, was struck by a truck while riding her bicycle. She sustained a broken neck, a broken leg, and a massive, enclosed head injury. She was on a ventilator for a week and unconscious for another week.

Jennie began her slow journey back to reality with a small miracle. About two weeks after the accident, her mother entered her ICU room and said, "Jennie, Mommy needs a hug."

With her one free arm, Jennie responded with a real hug. From there she progressed to indicating yes and no with her fingers, appropriately squeezing our hands on command, and then whispering one word replies. Finally she was talking in whispered sentences.

Her grandfather asked her when she would begin to talk in a real voice and she said, "As soon as I figure out how!"

With daily occupational and physical therapy she slowly came back to us.

Jennie had been in fifth grade at a nationally-acclaimed charter school before the accident. Unfortunately the school was not equipped to deal with a brain-injured student. However, two months after the accident, a decision was made to have her return to school half days, primarily to create a more normal life for her. She would begin the process by re-socialization with her peers rather than intense academic work. Her therapies continued.

It was at this time that Sister Kizzie began private tutoring with her in an attempt to determine her learning potential. Sister would need every tool in her teaching arsenal together with an abundance of patience and persistence to figure out how to teach a child recovering from an injured and irritable brain. Fortunately, Sister Kizzie has a very scientific mind and became fascinated with observing the dynamics of a brain which was relearning and rechanneling around a damaged area.

Jennie's attention span was extremely limited. To keep her on task, Sister Kizzie would set the kitchen timer beginning with thirty seconds and gradually prolonging her focused periods until a timer wasn't necessary. Brain damage often causes fidgeting. While many lessons could be done at the table, sometimes lessons were learned dancing around the living room.

Sister Kizzie found it intriguing how Jennie could work a complicated math problem in her head and come up with the correct answer, but was unable to write the step-by-step process on paper. Her memory constantly played tricks. She could remember, for example, that an hour had sixty minutes, but not that a minute had sixty seconds. Progress sometimes was astonishingly rapid; other times it was painstakingly slow.

Ten months after the accident a new school year was beginning. With Sister Kizzie's help and patience, Jennie had made tremendous progress. The decision was made to return her to the parish parochial school she had attended for her earlier grades. The setting was familiar to her; all the teachers knew her and were willing to work with her and Sister Kizzie. The faculty met with Sister and together they formulated an individual educational plan for Jennie.

Jennie's progress with Sister Kizzie had been so remarkable that it was decided she should try sixth grade. She attended school full time and continued the tutoring for two hours after school. Sixth grade was successful with Sister Kizzie helping as much with keeping Jennie organized as with intense tutoring.

By seventh grade, Jennie thought she could handle school alone, with the understanding that she could call on Sister as needed. She did that with some frequency.

Jennie is now in her senior year of high school. She has done very well academically. She sings in two choirs and heads the Speech and Debate Team at her school.

There is no doubt that her success is in large part due to the intense tutoring by Sister Kizzie during the long process of healing and retraining an injured brain. The family is eternally grateful for Sister Kizzie's skills and her generous spirit.

*Sister Kizzie kept the family informed about Jennie and her progress. In 2004 she wrote to the family.*

Jennie got her neck brace off last week. What a relief for her! It makes her look much better. She has only been going to school half days since Christmas. One afternoon a week she still

*Emily, Jennie, Amy, and Michael in 2010*

has therapy. Three days a week I pick her up at noon and tutor her, hoping she can be caught up by fall with all she either forgot or missed.

Jennie is actually doing quite well academically. She can figure out things and remember, but it just takes a little longer. That part of the brain is where most of the damage happened. But kids' brains repair themselves. They make new brain cells. I wish the rest of us could make new brain cells too, as we start getting slower and more forgetful.

Sometimes Jennie acts like a five or six-year-old instead of her twelve years. But that will come in time. The doctors told us, "Don't expect this to happen soon. Think of a year or so."

### Jennie's Thanksgiving Prayer

*After Jennie was home and recovering, the family had an open house to personally thank the many generous people. Sister Kizzie and Amy read a poem about volunteers and had a thanksgiving prayer service.*

## Volunteers

Many will be shocked to find,
When the day of judgment nears,
That there's a special place in heaven,
Set aside for volunteers.
Furnished with big recliners,
Satin couches and footstools,
Where there are no committee chairmen,
No yard sales or rest area coffee to serve,
No library duty or bulletin assembly.
There will be nothing to print or staple
Not one thing to fold or mail.
Telephone lists will be outlawed.
But a finger snap will bring
Cool drinks and gourmet dinners
And rare treats fit for a king.
You ask, "Who'll serve these privileged
And work for all they're worth?"
Why, all those who reaped the benefits,
And not once volunteered on earth.

*Anonymous*

Blessed be this place where we have gathered.
   Light our way as we journey. *Light candle one.*
   Light our way with gratitude. *Light candle two.*
   Light our way with love. *Light candle three.*
We have invited you here to join us in gratitude, to receive our thanks. It is easy to say thank you when all goes well, and when we receive just what we want – the nice and the good. Thanksgiving is a prayer, a prayer offered for everything given – the good and the bad.

We are all aware of the ten lepers who were healed by Jesus. Only one came back to thank Jesus, to present himself to the One who helped him, and pay his debt of gratitude. We, too, wish to say thank you and express our gratitude.

God sends each person into this world with a special message to deliver, with a special song to sing for others, with a special act of love to bestow. Tragedy hit our family. All of you have helped us to get through this and to go on. And we are grateful.

We'll all meet together again in heaven some day. Thank you for your generosity while here on earth. Let us close with the Blessing of St. Francis.

May the Lord bless you and keep you.

May He show His face to you and have mercy.

May He turn His countenance toward you and give you peace.

May the Lord bless you.

## Ndoleleji, Tanzania

*In January 2008, Father Danny Ohmann invited his two sisters, Sister Kizzie and Janet, and Roy and me to teach in the secondary school in Ndoleleji, Tanzania. Arriving at the school, we were excited to see a new classroom building and another dormitory under construction. Our excitement was quickly diminished when we visited with the second headmaster. The first headmaster was on medical leave leaving only four teachers for more than 400 students of all ages.*

*Returning to the states, Sister Kizzie wrote about Africa in the Franciscan Sisters' Community Newsletter.*

In January 2008, I had the opportunity and privilege to visit my brother, Daniel Ohmann, M.M. in Tanzania, Africa. One experience was to visit and camp out with the Watatulu, a tribe which Father Danny has been working with for some years. They are a wandering or nomadic tribe along the Rift Valley where there is vegetation to feed the cattle. Cows are their wealth as well as their bank. They don't have money but they may trade a cow for something they need. The Watatulu are very private. They do not mingle much with other tribes. The one blessing for this way of life is that AIDS is rare.

As we drove up to this Watatulu village and the compound and the small hut which the people built for Father Danny, I was feeling right at home. The land looked just like the Tohono O'odham Reservation west of Tucson where I once lived with Sister Ange Mayers.

*Father's Danny's compound with the Watatulu*

At Mass on Sunday, one of the men began singing. I thought for a moment that I was back on the Reservation as he sounded just like one of the O'odham song leaders. After Mass they asked us each to say a few words. I told them how their land and their singing made me feel at home. They were so happy to know that there are similarities, and therefore con-nections between the tribes in Africa and

*Sister Kizzie retrieving a ball in the field*

the tribes in North America.

The highlight of the stay was teaching English in the local secondary school in Ndoleleji, the village where Father Danny lives when he is not with the Watatulu. Totally prepared, I had lesson plans,

*Father Danny, Sister Kizzie and Janet at Mass*

chalk, charts, and props. As I looked over the students, I said to myself, "This feels good."

It had been a long time since I stood in front of a group of students. Within five minutes I realized that my way was not working. So much for lesson plans. I told them a little about my country and asked if they understood my English. They looked at me as though I was not only from another country but another planet. I knew that I needed to change so I put away all lesson plans, and made up the lesson as I went along. It was apparent that they were not accustomed to being asked questions. They would hear a lecture and then copy all the notes from the chalkboard into their exercise books. For homework they should memorize them. I told them that I expected them to

*Students waiting at the secondary school*

209

speak in English, as speaking the language was the only way to learn. It didn't help while in the classroom, but outside, they spoke freely.

The students had no books and the teachers each had one. I saw several dictionaries in a locked storeroom. I asked one of the teachers if we could use them, explaining that a dictionary was the most important book for learning a language. He had no key to open the door. Only the headmaster had a key and he was not in that week. As the days went on and I learned more about their educational system, I felt sorry for them. I wondered how they could ever learn. The percentage of students passing their national exam is low. However, there are some students who learn. They hunger for knowledge.

I found the elementary school to be better organized and more disciplined than the high school. But it was also very sad as they had very few supplies.

One morning as I walked around the school grounds, I saw a group of first graders sitting on the gravel walkway very busy writing numbers from 1 to 9 in the sand. The teacher explained to me that those who had mastered writing the numbers in the sand with their fingers could go back into the classroom.

I walked over to the classroom. All the students came rushing to the door. The numbers were neatly written on the board so I said them in English. They all repeated what I said. I don't know if they will remember them, but they were entertained. While they waited for their classmates to return, they just sat on the floor talking to each other. There were no desks for the little ones. Only the upper grades had desks.

There were ten teachers and more than 700 students in this elementary school. Students spent so much of the day with no supervision. I asked the teachers how they could manage so many students. They said they were fortunate that they had so many teachers. Most schools had less.

*After teaching, we reflected on our experiences in Father Danny's newsletter to family and benefactors.*

*Sister Kizzie taught English.* While visiting Ndoleleji, I was granted the opportunity to teach English at the secondary school. It was a good

*Sister Kizzie teaching English*

experience and an adventure. Having taught for many years, I was well prepared with lesson plans. Within a few minutes I realized the students were accustomed to a methodology different from mine. I quickly changed to their way of learning.

Some students were very eager and ready to learn despite the conditions. There were no books. Each student copied notes from the blackboard into their exercise books. Most students had very neat penmanship.

The students learned some English, though I did not learn any Sukuma.

*Janet Haas taught Biology and Sex Education.* Teaching at the secondary school in Ndoleleji for a week was quite an experience. I'm not sure who learned more: the students, Father Danny, my interpreter, or my-

*Father Danny and Janet on sex education*

self. I'm hoping the students got a more complete picture of the functioning and care of their bodies so they stay healthier. Whatever these students are learning, it is against great odds. Classrooms are overcrowded, supplies are limited, teachers are scarce and in need of more training. The people of Africa need to be commended for their effort.

*Roy and I taught Introduction to Computers.* "Speak English!" The teacher told the assembly early morning at the secondary school. "That's why you are here."

That proved to be very difficult for more than a hundred African students who were seeing a computer for the first time. After a day of introducing terminology and basic concepts, we connected cables to the truck's battery and powered up a computer. In a matter of minutes our class of twenty doubled in size. In their eighteen or more years, many of these Africans had never seen a cell phone, iPod, or television set.

Is it any wonder that in their excitement they started speaking Swahili?

*Teaching computers*

## Yarnell, Arizona

*In 1985 Sister Kizzie went to Yarnell, Arizona for about a year to minister to orphans with the Friends of Our Little Brothers. Yarnell is a beautiful place in the mountains northwest of Phoenix. Her daily Communion service, enhanced on special days such as Ash Wednesday, soon became very popular.*

*Sister Kizzie taught the students conversational English and prepared them for the high school equivalency test and for the TOEFL, an English test for foreign students. She also taught Spanish to the faculty. Sister Kizzie did some individual tutoring, particularly in composition, and helped students with the school newspaper which was written in English. She organized and supervised field trips.*

*Sister Kizzie lived and worked closely with students. She helped them with community living, ate with them, played volley ball or pool with them. She says her most important duty was talking to the students and just being there for them.*

### Nuestros Pequenos Hermanos

This is a gift for you from us, Nuestros Pequenos Hermanos, because you have been very kind and because you have been sharing your time, your home, and your family.

This little remembrance is our way to THANK YOU for your help.

*A card from the Yarnell students*

213

*Part Four*

THANKS SISTER ELIZABETH.

I WISH THAT YOU
WILL BE HERE, BUT IT
CAN NOT BE TRUE BECAUSE
YOU HAVE TO LEAVE.
IN THIS LIFE EACH
ONE HAS HIS OWN WAY
AND IT IS YOUR DECISION.
I ADMIRE YOUR GREAT
HEART AND GENEROSITY
THAT YOU SHARED WITH US.
I'M NEVER GOING TO FORGET
THESE NICE THINGS BECAUSE
YOU ARE ON MY MIND AND I
JUST WANT TO SAY
THANK FOR YOU PATIENCE,
UNDERSTANDING, AND LOVE.
I HOPE THAT ONE DAY
I WILL SEE YOU AGAIN
BUT HOW I WISH THAT
EVERYTHING WILL BE FINE,
IN YOUR LIFE,
I WILL MISS YOU.

GOD BLESS YOU.

. . . . . . . . . . . . .

WITH ALL OUR LOVE.
MIGUEL & JOSE VELASCO.

*From students in the English class in Yarnell*

214

# Part Five
# Reflections

We are all born into one human family,
baptized into one Christian Church.
We are all God's children,
all brothers and sisters.
Sister Kizzie, 2003

*During her sixty years as a Franciscan Sister, Sister Kizzie wrote about her vocation, her beliefs and principles, her challenges and her rewards. Part Five includes reflections on her childhood, on being a sister and a missioner, and on living in a global community, and stories about her sabbatical at the Catholic Theological Union in Chicago.*

## A Rich Family Life

*Born the seventh of eight children to John and Elizabeth Ohmann on March 9, 1933 in Greenwald, Minnesota, Sister Kizzie was baptized Elizabeth. After my mother, Mabel, five boys (Abbie, Jackie, Ermie, Danny, and Ruby) and a five-year wait, she was a welcomed baby girl. Two and a half years later, her youngest sister, Janet, was born.*

### Judging and Misjudging

A simple action can cause reactions. Mom was a great cook. The dinner was good, and having company made it even better. Peach sauce was often served after a very full meal. Mom told us that if we finish everything on our plates, we could have ice

215

*Grandma and Grandpa Ohmann at our wedding in 1964*

*Sister Kizzie in pigtails and plaid*

cream in the afternoon. Janet couldn't finish her peaches. I whispered to her that I would finish her peaches. We exchanged her full dish and my empty dish, thinking no one would see us.

My aunt saw us and said to my mother, "Every family has one with a sweet tooth."

Mom just shook her head. Now everyone in our family knew that I was not the one with the sweet tooth. In my eleven-year-old mind, I wondered why my aunt made such a judgment without even knowing me. I was very upset, but finished the peaches and

216

went outdoors to sit by the side of the house to think. This was my first conscious reflection on the difference between judging and misjudging.

It was also my first awareness of the nearness of God, knowing that He was aware of the truth.

*Kizzie attended grade school at St. Andrew's School in Greenwald and at Sacred Heart School in Freeport. Following one year at Melrose High School, she finished her high school education at St. Francis in Little Falls, Minnesota.*

## Accepting God's Forgiveness

We, as faith-filled people, have such a richness and wealth in our background. It goes back to the very beginning of time. As people grew in their understanding of what it meant to be faith-filled, they began to write it down. This helped people realize that there was a God, that God was leading them, and that God would always be there for them no matter what they did. God asked Jeremiah in the Old Testament to remind the people that He was there for them. He said, "I will forgive their sins and I will no longer remember their wrongs." 31:34b.

God is ready to forgive us. We read in The Prodigal Daughter written by Jeffrey Archer, that God constantly asks us, "Are you ready – ready to accept My forgiveness? I want to give you My forgiveness. Are you ready to accept it?"

All this is so easy to say, so easy to talk about, but difficult to act upon. Actually, it's *very* difficult. God is God, a spirit, a spiritual being. We are humans, from a different world. We can only think and talk in terms of what we know and understand. That means that I really have to see and experience forgiveness from others as well as offer forgiveness to others to understand that God will act in the same manner.

*Ribbons and a pretty smile*

Very early in my life, in my childhood, I was given an insight into forgiveness. My sister and I were enjoying a bowl of ice cream, a real treat in those days. She finished hers before I did. Then she very nicely reached over and took a spoonful of mine. My reaction was anything but godlike, or even ladylike, not even nice. I threw my spoon at her. Of course, that brought tears, and Mom to the rescue.

Mom didn't even require an apology. But she required us to clean up the spilled ice cream that never made it to my sister's mouth and the spattering of ice cream from the spoon I threw. She also required a promise that we would not just take anything from someone else, and that we would learn to share.

Moms can be very much like God. She could overlook the incident, help clean up the mess, and help us act like brothers and sisters to each other again. In this example I had to both forgive and accept forgiveness. With my sister that wasn't too hard, especially with Mom helping us understand that both of us had a part in it. But then I was pretty angry at the same time. To me that brought God into the picture. How could God forgive me for getting angry? After some reflection on what had happened, and more reflection on the fact that there were no great repercussions from my sister or from Mom, I began to realize that it was enough for God that I say, "I'm sorry. I'll be more careful next time."

He forgave me. I knew it in my heart.

God never forces, just waits for us to let God be God. This incident was something small and childish. As we grow older, our actions become bigger and more serious. As Mom used to say, "With little kids, there are little problems. With big kids, there are big problems."

Our problems, our sins, become more serious as we grow older. Our acceptance of forgiveness has to become bigger too. It helps to think of God as growing along with us. Actually it is our understanding of God which grows. Either way, we grow with God. So if He forgives small sins, He is

*The 'little girls' Janet and Kizzie with Ermie*

*The 'girls' today with Jackie and Abbie*

219

*Sister Kizzie's family at her parents' 60ᵗʰ Wedding Anniversary. Back row: Ermie, Jackie, and Ruby. Middle row: Abbie, Mabel, Sister Kizzie, Father Danny, and Janet. Seated: Grandpa and Grandma.*

just as ready to forgive big sins.

Once a lady told me that it was years after she had an abortion that she was able to tell anyone, especially God, what she had done. And even after she said it, asking God for forgiveness was hard. Only when she started babysitting, caring for a baby she never had, did she realize that God had forgiven her. In her heart she knew. He was giving her another chance. It may not be her own baby she was caring for, but she was doing what God wanted her to do. She accepted forgiveness. Her heart was at peace.

God is so merciful. His mercy is beyond our understanding. Faith tells us it is there. The peace in our hearts tells us it is real. Psalm 103 tells us, "As far as the east is from the west, so far does He remove our sins from us." So great is His mercy and love.

*Grandpa and Grandma Ohmann died in 1981, my mother, Mabel, in 1992, Ruby in 1997, and Ermie in 2008. Sister Kizzie was diagnosed with uterine cancer in 2005 and has recovered wonderfully. In 2008, the Most Reverend Gerald Kicanas, Bishop of Tucson, included the following memo in his weekly letter to the Diocese. It isn't everyone who can read his or her death notice!*

### Remember in Your Prayers

Please pray for the repose of the soul of Sister Elizabeth Ohmann, OSF, who died June 7, 2008 at St. Francis Convent in Little Falls, Minnesota. In her 66 years of religious life, Sister served in Rome, Ghana, Nigeria, Egypt, Belgium, Minnesota, Alabama and in our Diocese, most recently at St. Pius X Parish in Tucson. The Funeral Mass was celebrated June 11.

*This was followed by another email. In the meantime, I'm sure many people were deeply saddened by the Bishop's news.*

Our sincere apologies to Sister Elizabeth Ohmann for the incorrect information in today's memo. Sister Elizabeth sent a death notice for Sister Sheila Mortonson, OSF, who died June 7, 2008. The item inadvertently and mistakenly listed Sister Elizabeth as having passed away. Sister Elizabeth is still very much with us. Thanks be to God!

## Being a Sister and a Missioner

*On July 31, 1951, Kizzie was accepted into the novitiate of the Franciscan Sisters of Little Falls. She chose the name Sister Miriam. In 1967, Sister Miriam changed her name to Sister Elizabeth, a privilege granted to the religious by the Ecumenical Council. Friends and relatives were pleased because she would*

*With my mother Mabel, Grandma, Grandpa, Janet, and Jackie at the convent in Little Falls*

*again be called by a favorite nickname, Sister Kizzie. Grandnieces in Tucson call her Aunt Sister, a name coined by their mother Amy.*

## A Real Nun

Emily, my grandniece, at about age five, asked me, "Aunt Sister, are you a real nun?"

"Yes, I am." I responded. "Where did you hear the word nun?"

She said that she didn't know. "I must have heard someone say it."

That didn't surprise me. Once Emily hears a word, she remembers it. Then I asked, "Do you know what a nun is?"

With certainty, she said, "Yes, I do. Number one. She never gets married."

"That's right."

"Number two. She prays a lot."

"I hope so." I said.

"And number three. She's very old."

*In January 2002, Sister Kizzie responded to an article entitled 'Women of God' published in the <u>Atlantic Monthly</u>. She attributes the evolution of the religious life today to Divine Providence.*

## Always Will There be Nuns

I found 'Women of God' most interesting. I love the expression – endangered species. I have not thought of myself as endangered, though we often talk about the religious life as we know it to be dying out. I went with my niece Sarah once to look for and count a certain plant which is now on the endangered species list. These plants and animals are by law protected. So far no one has given any special protection to nuns!

In the first part of the article the author gave a very stereotypical picture of nuns. We were described as "teaching, comforting, visiting, cooking" – saying what we did, not actually who we were. Her early experiences with nuns were very limited. Yet she described nuns as though one description represented all nuns.

The author's description though is the usual stereotype, the way most people saw nuns before the 1960s. Many still hold this view and wonder why some nuns are not living up to it.

My early experiences with nuns and teachers were not at all as described in the article. The author seems to remember the worst, while I remember the best. My experiences were all very positive.

The author says it took many years and a happy accident of meeting three nuns that brought her close enough to have conversations with them. I wonder if that was when she first saw nuns as people. Maybe if she had allowed herself to get to know them in her early years, she would have felt differently. That is easy to say. There may never have been the opportunity for her to do that. Many nuns never gave children a chance to get to know them.

We are facing the demise of a way of life as we have known it. But I have the faith to believe that this is all in the Providence of God. The way of life for nuns is in an evolutionary spurt. It has been happening all along, but never as drastically or dramatically as now. Nuns have always been in the foreground for beginning new works, for expressing new ideas, for questioning the values and practices of the Church.

The author gives some very good examples of these. Her entire description of nuns today was very well done, from poverty, celibacy, prayer life, differences between contemplative and active communities to post Vatican II traditional, transitional and updated communities. She covered the entire gamut.

There will always be nuns. Though the form by which they live and serve cannot be guessed.

## Many Dilemmas

Do I attend certain events, which at times can be expensive, when the people I work with can't do so?

Do I live with more conveniences and more comfortably than the people I serve?

Since I work side-by-side with Mexicans on the same staff, should I be earning a higher salary than they do because we are used to a higher standard of living and because it is more expensive to live in the United States? How is a just salary determined, judged, or justified? Should those who have fewer needs receive a smaller salary?

Sharing many cultures has made me appreciate other ways of living, for example, other kinds of foods. More important to me is the availability of food, especially when so many do not have any.

My values are not in material things. The money I spend does not go much beyond the necessities of life. I weigh carefully all expenditures, such as movies, cultural events, car use, and so on. If I say that I work with the poor and for the poor, I should live as they do. At times, the common good takes over my personal preferences. At times, the actual money I spend is a bit more than a lower-priced similar article because higher values such as dignity and justice to the workers are more important that the money spent.

How do I spend my time? Time is precious, and often free time is little. Do I use it freely and alone? Do I use it to spend time looking around? In 2005 when I was diagnosed with uterine cancer, my superiors suggested that I take some time to just *be* for two months. Allow each moment to flow into the next without being concerned what the next moment would bring. Even cancer can bring gifts.

What is my reward? My reward is seeing people's hearts and minds open, indeed, do flip-flops, when they understand the realities of others.

## Responsibility for Gifts

Each person has a special work, a special talent, or a special gift given by God. Along with the special gift comes privilege. And this privilege carries along with it responsibility. I have been given, therefore, I need to give accordingly.

The Virgin Mary is our example in carrying this out. The one thing she did is also the one thing we are asked to do. Christ must be born in every soul and formed in every life. She bore Christ as a human being into this world. We now have the responsibility to bear Christ into this world by being the hands, the voice, the feet, and the compassion of Christ today.

## On her Fiftieth Anniversary

Fifty years! Who would ever believe it! I was always considered one of the two little Ohmann girls. I think these two girls have not only grown up, but have gotten older.

Fifty years! It does not seem very long ago when I had the feeling that God was trying to tell me something. I had no idea what He had in mind. I barely knew what I had in mind.

I wasn't in the convent long when one of the boys came to Little Falls with Mom and Pa to visit. I think it was Ruby, but it actually sounds like Jackie. They were ready to leave when he said to me, "I will give you a dollar if you come home with us."

I don't know what kind of look I gave him, but I do remember saying, "It would cost a lot more than a dollar to take me home with you."

They didn't take me along and now fifty years later, I can say that I'm glad I didn't go with them that day. A lot has happened during that period of time. As in any way of life, married, single, or religious, there are good days and there are hard days. Somehow we live through both kinds. We can remember both.

St. Paul reminds us that we are called for freedom. This freedom gives me the opportunity to make choices. So my choice is to concentrate on the good and all the blessings that I have received. I say what God said when he created the world. He looked at it and said, "It is good."

He said this each day after He made something new. "It is good."

Each evening I wonder what good or what blessing God has given me that day. What do I have to be thankful for this day? For what can I say, "It is good?" Each evening I write this into my little Thank You Book.

Today I don't have any trouble seeing the good. I look at all of you here and I am grateful. I say, "Look at all the beauty which God created and it is right here."

All of us helped Him create the beauty. I think He is saying today too, "It is good."

After God created man and woman, He did not only say, "It is good." He said, "It is *very* good!"

We all know that not all days are good. Some days it is a struggle to find the blessings. I often think of the time I lived on the Tohono O'odham Reservation west of Tucson with Sister Ange Mayers, who is originally from New Munich, Minnesota. One day we were walking from the church across the yard to the hall. The Reservation is on the driest and most barren part of the Sonoran Desert. There was not much in the yard between the church and the hall except sand and dust and dirt. As we walked across, we both suddenly stopped and stared at a spot on the ground and yelled, "A flower! A yellow flower!"

We stooped, picked it, and admired it, showing it to all those around us. I'm sure everyone else wondered what had happened to us. I think I did hear a side remark, "They've been in the desert too long. Too much sun."

Actually we learned to see beauty and appreciate it in a tiny yellow flower. It was good. St. Francis would have been proud of us. We are free to see a barren desert or a flower. It's a choice.

Jesus tried to teach the Apostles to serve through love. In the Gospel we heard that the Apostles wanted to call down fire from heaven to burn up all the people because the Samaritans wouldn't let them and Jesus stay in their town. The Samaritans had their reasons. Jesus was a Jew, a stranger, a foreigner, and He was on his way to Jerusalem. These were all good reasons not to welcome Him.

Jesus reacted very differently than the Apostles. He turned around, talked to the strangers, and was not only willing to help them but even invited some to follow Him.

Jesus sends an invitation to every person. Thank God He invites each of us to do something different. It would be a boring world if each one of us wanted to do the same thing. What if everybody wanted to be a potato farmer? Who would pick them and distribute them? After eating nothing but potatoes for a few days, who would want to eat them?

Jesus invites each one to do something special. I believe I have been called to work among people of different cultures. I acquaint myself with their customs and try to adapt to living their way. Often our ways are very different. To them theirs are good. To us ours are good. Both are good.

This is an example of how I think we are each called to something special. When I was working in Peru among the Aymara People on the Altiplano, Father Danny came to visit. As he was leaving, he asked me how I could stay there. Everything seemed so hopeless.

Later I got to know the place and people where he worked and lived in Tanzania and I wondered how he could stay there. Everything seemed so hopeless.

Probably neither of us really knows the answer. But we know in our hearts our response would be, "It is good."

Each one of us is called. Each one of us has a specific job to do. We respond to that which we believe in our hearts Jesus has called us to do. It is good.

Today we are called to be here and to celebrate, to enjoy each other. It is good.

## A Letter to Laura

*In 1999 Laura, the wife of Sister Kizzie's nephew Peter, sought advice as she had been thinking about becoming a Catholic for a long time but just wasn't quite sure. She had been receiving Holy Communion even though she was not formally a member of the Church. This made her a bit uncomfortable since she was helping with church work at the University in Las Cruces. Laura was worried that the parishioners would find out that she wasn't Catholic, but was receiving Communion. Sister Kizzie told her that if she worked at the church with Catholics, she could also eat at the table with Catholics.*

There is nothing I would like better than to accompany you on your spiritual journey. You have greatly honored me. I have no doubts at all that you have put a lot of thought and prayer into these concerns. I struggle with some of these same issues all the time. Most of my work now is among those who are not Catholic. Even the word Catholic is of concern to me. If we change the capital C to small c and use catholic, we mean universal, inclusive of everyone. We say it every time we say the Creed. As Catholics, we think we are the only ones who know what is right. We tend to think of catholic only with the capital C and forget that it means universal. What is it? Pride or possessiveness of Jesus?

You are a very sensitive person and are developing a very sensitive conscience. The Catholic Church has always been very good about using guilt for anything a person does that the Church does not like or agree with. Now I'm finding out that the Catholic Church is not the only one. Those in the Protestant Church tell me they thought they had the monopoly on guilt. I'm finding that those in the Catholic Church who write the rules and regulations aren't always right or maybe I should say that I think they are making different rules than Jesus would have if He were here now. If I'm reading Jesus right, a lot of us are imposters.

What I'm really trying to say is that I feel bad that you think maybe you are living a lie. I don't think you are. Nor are you a thief. We do not have a monopoly on Jesus. Most of this is a matter of legalities and I don't think that we can just ignore them. It puts you in a very awkward position, but I think the Spirit is very much alive and active through all this. I have the faith and strongly believe that this is one little step that is leading to a greater and all-encompassing church.

I didn't mean to get so wordy about this. It is so important. I am very proud and humbled that you would invite me into your life in this way. You will know and feel when you are ready to

*Laura with husband Peter*

join the Church. You will not have doubts as you do now. We can talk about it further.

Until then, don't let the guilties keep you from Jesus. Jesus invites all to the table. There is no one more open and longing for our friendship than Jesus. I will pray for guidance for both of us.

## Living in a Global Community

In the Gospel we hear Jesus telling us that we should go to all nations and make disciples. I guess I took that quite literally and went. Now the world has become a global community. We don't have to go to other countries to meet people who appear to be different than we are, who act differently, and who do different things. Many are different and strange, yes, but so interesting and exciting. Once we start exchanging and sharing, we find that neither one is better – just different.

For example, is bread better than tortillas or are tortillas better than bread? It depends on what you are used to or maybe on your taste buds. And taste buds can be developed.

Time is another dimension which is looked at differently by many people. I was born and raised in an area where everyone, including me, spoke German. We are hard workers and we like things done on time. For most of us, it meant our livelihood. We had to plant in the spring, depending on the rain. God helped us keep our schedule and we were very rigid about it. Not only that, convent life kept me very scheduled too. Actually you could have set your watch by what I did. Everything was always on time. Then I went to Peru, as a missionary. Being a very scheduled person, I wanted our meetings there to begin on time. I quickly learned that no one way was better than the other.

I also learned that we are not so very different from people of other nations. We actually share more likenesses than we do differences. The differences are material and passing. For example, is it better to have shelter in a mud hut with a thatched roof, or shelter in a house of lumber or bricks with a tile roof or shingles? The rain and hot sun will stay out either way. Is it better to wear a coat with sleeves or a poncho? So much doesn't really make any difference.

I began seeing similarities with little variations. We all eat, sleep, work, play, pray, have music, and are able to think. Mothers from all over are concerned about their babies. Fathers support their families. Children depend on their parents. We all enjoy visiting with family and friends. We share humanity.

We are all born into one human family, baptized into one Christian Church. We are all God's children, all brothers and sisters.

*Sister Kizzie often said that Christmas is her favorite time of the year – with the anticipation and expectation of something about to happen during the season of Advent, and the surprise and greatness of its fulfillment at Christmas. She wrote about Christmas in a 2002 Franciscan Sisters' Community Newsletter.*

## Adapting to the Local

Become one with the people with whom you live and work! An important consideration I read about and learned many years ago as I was thinking about and hoping to become a missionary in a foreign country with different customs from my own.

Now in the Sonoran Desert of the Southwest the idea of adapting has turned to the Christmas tree. Local trees and plants have become Christmas trees. In 1990 we used a tree branch.

During the Advent and Christmas season in 1994, I lived on the O'odham Reservation in Pisinimo, Arizona. After Sister Ange Mayers looked around one afternoon for the right tree, we found it in the driveway of our own home – a tumbleweed!

In 1999, our Christmas tree in Tucson was the dried blossom of the century plant. Two years later I used the dried blossom of the yucca plant. This year my Christmas tree is the dried branch of the fruit of the date palm.

## The Journey of the Magi

Over the past week, I have found myself thinking about the three figures that represent the Magi in my nativity set. The Gospel introduces us to these mysterious characters known as the wise ones from the East who studied the stars. I have come to a conclusion that we, as people of faith, can see ourselves in the journey of the Magi. In a very profound sense our journeys mirror theirs.

It is not hard to imagine the many difficulties and dangers that could have been a part of the Magis' journey. Did their friends and families support their travels? Perhaps their colleagues tried to discourage them. The travelers no doubt encountered unbearable heat during the day and very cold nights in the desert. There was the ever present danger of bandits.

And yet, the Magi felt obligated to answer the call of the Star of Bethlehem. The travelers, above all difficulty and danger, sought to share their gifts with the newborn Jesus. The story of the Magi is perhaps a foreshadowing of the story of Jesus who, above all difficulty and danger, sought to share His gifts with us.

This Christmas I learned something from the figures that journey toward the manger. Our journeys as people of faith are often filled with difficulty and danger. There is frustration when it seems that our prayers go unanswered. There is discouragement when our work is misinterpreted as aiding and abetting. There are times when we are physically exposed to intense heat and dangerous plants and wildlife in the desert. There are times when we must endure pain, suffering, and death. There are times when we seek affirmation.

In spite of their many challenges, the Magi faithfully offered themselves and their gifts to another. Having met the little baby Jesus, the Magi were changed individuals. Their lives took on new direction as they traveled home another way. Is this not true of us as well? We become changed individuals when we share and experience the person of Jesus in another.

May God's many blessings guide you every step of your journey. Merry Christmas!

## On Freedom and Justice

Consider the word freedom. In the United States we have used that word in many contexts. The Pledge of Allegiance to the Flag states "... with liberty (freedom) and justice for all." For some of us, freedom has been taken for granted. I thought that was the same for everybody. My world was small, so I thought everybody's world was small. At age eight, World War II opened a world of which I had little or no awareness.

At age 11, for doing what I thought was a good deed, I was misjudged and misconstrued. Not knowing it, I did my first theological reflection. I could not feel guilty for something that someone else thought was not good, when I knew in my own heart it was good. An inner freedom allowed me to judge myself.

Our way of life, customs, the culture – all led to a reserved, puritanical way of thinking. My newly reflected freedom could not be openly discussed or shared. Only Mom seemed to have an insight but also could not encourage my development of this thinking. It didn't fit.

Introduction to racism opened another door. Native Americans and Blacks were taken for granted and their places in society were taken for granted. That is what the books told us and that is what educated people told us. Yet I wondered why I could have a good house and a good education and they couldn't. The poor pagan babies in China needed to be ransomed. We were made to feel we were the only ones who could do it because we had a few pennies and they didn't. Justice, with freedom, began to enter into my way of thinking.

A consciousness of freedom and justice was not developed or encouraged. That is just the way things were. Acceptance was a virtue. The expression became: "It all depends on where you were born." I had become a victim of the times, a staunch believer in "This is as it is. This is as it should be." Even Vatican II was going against what had always been. No way would I be a part of the new when the old was good.

Deep inside the desire to ransom pagan babies and convert the world smoldered a spark in the ashes. Latin America opened as a great mission field. Religious communities were encouraged to send 10% of their personnel. It was not China and pagan babies, but it was mission territory – adventure and souls to be saved. For five years my dream again was not encouraged or developed.

Then a door opened. My destination was Peru. Another language, people, customs, clothing, food, religious expression, and time, all took on a different meaning, opening new avenues. My way was not the only right way. Their ways had been lived probably longer than my ways, so why weren't they right too? No longer was it a question. They were right too!

Time had become the pivotal point. After two years of

listening, observing, and learning, time became the NOW. Now is the important time. What I do now is of importance. What freedom that gave me. Worrying about a schedule, being on time, getting something done, and being somewhere aren't of importance. Who is here right now, or what is being done right now, are to be valued.

Demetrius Dumm, in an explanation of the Exodus, revisited the idea of freedom. The real miracle of the Exodus happened in the minds and hearts of the people. It restored confidence and freedom. God gave ten guidelines to the use of freedom. Freedom was not created but recreated, as was my Latin American sense of time and freedom, which had been lost in the hectic life of the United States.

## On Sabbatical at the Catholic Theological Union

*In 2001 Sister Kizzie took a break from her work on the border to accept a sabbatical at the Hesburgh Center in Chicago. She chose the highly-recommended Catholic Theological Union to spend time away from the everyday concerns and stresses of work. You will appreciate and enjoy her sense of humor as she writes about the program and her time spent in Chicago.*

I have chosen the Catholic Theological Union because it is a holistic, community-based, academic program, promoting spiritual and emotional development. Its basic assumption that we are on the way to becoming a World Church was inviting, as I am constantly in a multicultural atmosphere and our work encompasses much reflection on the global economy. Hopefully this is leading us to a united world.

In the course of these months my hope was to re-energize my body and deepen my personal relationship with God, renew the contemplative dimension of my life, and grow by input, study, prayer, and community. The program is the answer to my prayer to have more time alone. I have the opportunity to step back, reflect, and assess the activities and ministries in which I have been involved. It's a struggle to find time to reflect after a full day's work when my body is physically exhausted.

I'm enjoying being a student again, although this isn't exactly being a student as we have no exams or papers to do. I received a student ID which gets me into a lot of activities as well as the Lutheran Theology Library and McCormick School Libraries. When I put money on this card, I have access to the copy machine and the printer in the computer room. I can't decide where to keep this precious ID card. Guess I'll put in on a chain and carry it around my neck!

Two weeks into the program, I finally had phone and email service. The others told me to be happy about that as sometimes it takes three weeks or more.

Catholic Theological Union is an international community with hand-picked speakers from all over the world. Including the participants, I believe there are more than thirty countries represented. Every two days we have a different speaker updating us on issues of religion and the Church. No one wants to waste their time or our time, so each speaker gives us a whole course in two days. It sounds like a lot, and is a lot. The topics include Biblical Spirituality, Doing Theology, Introduction to Moral Theology, Fundamentals of Theology, The Prophets, Liturgy Ministries, communication and many others. One week we had Fundamentalism – not that they are trying to convert us but so we understand it better. Catholic Theological Union is anything but Fundamentalist.

Possessing a wealth of knowledge, the speaker on Liturgy Ritual was a terrific presenter and teacher, and had a knack for throwing in a side remark that was so funny. It was done so fast and cleverly that I would catch onto it a sentence or two later – after he had gone on to something else.

A missioner from Africa spoke on Faithfulness in a Multi-Religion World. His main point was that no one religion has all the answers. No one has all the truth. Everyone has a piece and all are called to holiness. We have been working that way for a long time. I told him that I was feeling a bit stifled here in a totally Catholic environment.

Then we had Demetrius Dumm, a Benedictine author, who spoke on Biblical Spirituality. Each sentence of his carried a lot of information, yet it was said so simply and full of humor. He would talk about something Jesus did and then he would say, "I wonder what Peter wrote in his diary that evening."

He'd laugh and say, "I can just see Peter sitting there chewing on the end of his beard and writing for the third day in a row, 'I don't understand this guy'."

Bishop Untener from Saganaw spoke to us. With the way he speaks it is no wonder he never got to a large diocese as Chicago or New York or Philadelphia. There sure is a lot of politics in the Church. If he wasn't as old as he is, he would probably be silenced. He said he knows Cardinal Ratzinger quite well and has been frequently called to his office. He may not speak very often, but he regularly writes and publishes articles.

Don Senior, the President of Catholic Theological Union, spoke on the Gospel of Mark. He is such a good teacher it is a shame his time has to be taken up as president. I was going to write some of the things he said, but I think I will just buy the tapes. I know it will not be quite the same as hearing him in person, but the message will be there.

Our last speaker talked about teaching a class, leading a meeting, or giving a homily. He gave us ways to read a section of the Bible, such as the Gospel for Sunday, and choose something to think about and apply it to our own lives today. It's amazing what he brought up.

One evening we walked over to Chicago University to hear a

panel on Religion and Violence against Women. The panel consisted of a Christian woman by the name of Rosemary Radford Ruether, a Jewish woman, and a Muslim woman. I have forgotten their names. Rosemary R is a big name in the feminist movement. However, she was the least impressive speaker. Actually she did not have a good delivery at all, and not a lot of content. The Jewish lady was good. The Muslim lady thought it was all right the way women are treated because the holy book says so. I think I'll stay at Catholic Theological Union. We have such great speakers there.

The bishop from Cheyene, Wyoming lives right here with us. In fact, I watch television with him. He is usually dressed in jeans and a T-shirt and introduces himself as Joe. He was here several days or perhaps a week before we found out he was a bishop.

One week I spoke at a luncheon for the faculty and students of the School for Global Ministries, a part of the Presbyterian School. I tried to sell the idea of attending a BorderLinks educational seminar. Hopefully I motivated them to send students to the border. Actually I was hoping to meet someone with some money to help us. I was not very optimistic about that though. The teachers in a Catholic school or any denomination – even in higher education, don't receive very high salaries. So I didn't really give that too much thought. I was so busy worrying about speaking to these highly educated people. They may be very educated but most of them don't have the life experiences that I've had with other cultures.

Thankfully the schedule allowed for private time and rest. I gave myself a delayed birthday present by going to the ballet. We saw three performances of the 20th Century Masters: Arpino's Viva Vivaldi, Tudor's Lilac Garden, and Massine's Les Presages. The first dancer came out on her toes and I don't think she stepped down on her whole foot for the first ten minutes. I was almost getting cramps in my legs. Each dancer must have a full time massage therapist!

One day I took a city bus to visit some sisters. I got on the bus and found a seat, making sure I was at a window so I could see the street signs to find the place to get off. We barely moved when everyone jumped up. Then I heard the driver saying, "Hustle! Hustle! Everyone get off! The bus is on fire!"

So I jumped up and hustled off the bus too. It smelled like brakes burning or maybe hot wires, but we saw no flames. The driver ran to find a phone. We stood on the sidewalk – not very smart as we were about five or six feet away from the bus. If the bus had burst into flames or exploded, we would have been in bad shape. After about ten minutes another bus came along and we continued on our way.

After I had dinner with the sisters, they gave me a ride home because they said it was not safe to take public transportation through this area at night by myself. I wasn't much concerned, but I gladly accepted the ride.

I really got quite spoiled here. My room was cleaned each week, somewhat superficially, but I didn't have to do it. I washed one of my windows just so I could look out and let the sun shine in. What a difference. The poor window was shocked at being so clean. I'll bet it was cold without the layers of dirt covering it.

A flock (if they're called flock) of parrots live in a park only a block from here. It seems a couple of parrots had escaped from a pet shop some years back, settled in the park, and adjusted to life in Chicago. Their nests look more like squirrels' nests than birds' nests. One nest is long, about the size of a bathtub, stretching along a branch. These parrots are a light green in color. They use their beaks when they walk along the branches just like the ones in zoos. I've only seen eight but I guess there are about twenty or more parrots in the park.

I will miss Chicago but am looking forward to a week of retreat in Notre Dame before heading back to Tucson.

*Sister Kizzie lived in the Spirit of St. Francis. She wrote this prayer while contemplating the plight of the migrants*

## The San Damiano Crucifix

The hands of Jesus on the San Damiano Crucifix are open, reaching out, loving, soft, and inviting all of us to come to Him. Hands, no longer in pain, but offering an invitation. Hands waiting for the response to be His hands, to be of assistance. I watch and pray for the moment to be those hands, to lift the weights, to ease the pain, to comfort, to listen, to give that cup of cold water in His name. Each day I see these moments as I hear of migrants crossing the border traveling through the desert, trying to find work to earn money to feed their families. Help me build the Kingdom by uniting people who have with people who do not have.

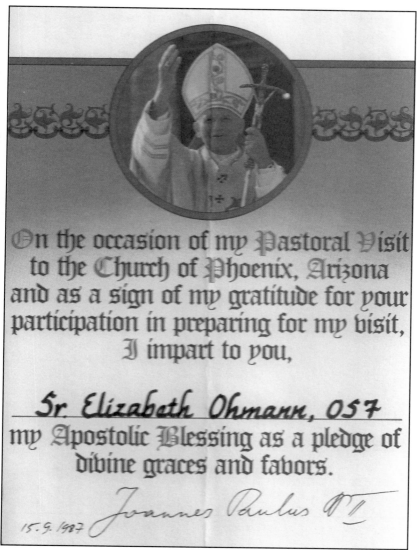

On the occasion of my Pastoral Visit to the Church of Phoenix, Arizona and as a sign of my gratitude for your participation in preparing for my visit, I impart to you,

*Sr. Elizabeth Ohmann, OSF*

my Apostolic Blessing as a pledge of divine graces and favors.

*Joannes Paulus PP II*

15.9.1987

*Apostolic Blessing from Pope John Paul II*

# PAPAL VISIT OFFICE
## Diocese of Phoenix – 1987
Most Reverend Thomas J. O'Brien, Bishop of Phoenix

DIOCESAN COORDINATOR
Fr. John J. McMahon
EVENTS COORDINATOR
Harvey Newquist
OPERATIONS COORDINATORS
Judy Wischer
Dr. Mary Jo French
DIOCESAN OFFICE
Msgr. Bernard Gordon
Sr. Dolores Tringl
Fr. James McFadden
Fr. Anthony Sotelo
CATECHESIS
Fr. Jack Spaulding
Anita Kildran
CIVIC AFFAIRS
Tommy Espinoza
COMMUNICATIONS
Marge Injasoulian
Chris Gunty
ECUMENISM
Msgr. Robert Donohoe
Fr. Edward Ryle
FINANCE
William Shover
HOSPITALITY
Sr. Bridget Henderson
Sr. Augusta Gaus
LITURGY
Fr. Dale Fushek
PROTOCOL
Fr. Richard W. Meyer
Fr. Robert Caruso
SECURITY
Larry Wetzel
SITES PREPARATION
Fr. Tim Davern
Bob Kohnen
SPECIAL SERVICES
Fr. Robert Wicht
Phyllis Vogelsang
TICKETS
Doug Sandahl
Fr. Cornelius Moynihan
TRANSPORTATION
Edward Murphy
USHERING
Arthur Aschauer
Jean Roozendaal
AIRPORT
Maj. Gen. Don Owens
Lt. Col. Jim Kzouth
ST. JOSEPH'S HOSPITAL
Jack Buckley
George Kazan
MOTORCADE
Ernie Mulholland
ST. MARY'S BASILICA
Fr. Warren Rouse
CIVIC PLAZA
Dr. Mary Jo French
C.H.A.
David Sauer
SS. SIMON & JUDE
Fr. Paul Smith
BISHOP'S HOUSE
John Author
NATIVE AMERICANS
Tony Machukay
Fr. Gilbert Hemauer
PAPAL MASS ASU
Jim O'Connell
MEDICAL SUPPORT
Dr. Glen Waterkotte
Dr. Fred Scott
ADMINISTRATIVE SECRETARY
Mary Holguin

Greetings:

When our Holy Father visited Phoenix last September he wished to give his special blessing to all those who helped prepare for his coming by their prayers, their time and their talents. Enclosed please find your copy of the Papal Blessing which he personally signed here in Phoenix on Tuesday morning the 15th before he left for Los Angeles. I hope you enjoy this gift of his.

From the Papal office may we also express our deepest gratitude for your help and sacrifices in preparing for the Holy Father's coming. May the gift of his presence among us endure throughout the new year.

May your heart be filled with the peace of Christ.

Father McMahon

UNITY IN THE WORK OF SERVICE – TO BUILD UP THE BODY OF CHRIST
400 East Monroe • Phoenix, Arizona 85004 • (602) 257-0030 • (602) 256-7919

*From the office of Most Reverend Thomas O'Brien, Bishop of Phoenix*

# About the Franciscan Sisters

The Franciscan Sisters of Little Falls, Minnesota, is a Roman Catholic Congregation of religious women founded in 1891 in central Minnesota by sixteen members of another Franciscan congregation. With the help of generous benefactors and land granted on the south side of Little Falls, the sisters constructed a building that immediately served as a convent, a residence for orphan children, a hospital, and a home for the aged. From these simple beginnings, the Franciscan Community flourished and continued to develop ministries in health care, education, and social services throughout the United States, South and Central America, and Africa.

According to their website at www.fslf.org, the community today has 166 sisters who have publicly professed the vows of poverty, chastity and obedience, consecrating their lives to God. In the spirit of St. Francis and St. Clare of Assisi, they serve the poor and marginalized people throughout the United States, Mexico, and Ecuador. Their joyful, creative, and steadfast spirit are their greatest gifts to the Church and to the world.

There are many opportunities to become a part of the Franciscan Sisters. The Franciscan Associates are lay women, men, and families from many walks of life who share a desire to live the Gospel with joy and zeal, and to share the spirit, charisma, and mission of the Franciscan Sisters. The Franciscan Community Volunteer program, open to single men and women of any faith tradition, entails a year of intentional community living, dedicated to serving and advocating on behalf of the underserved.

In addition one can join the more than 300 volunteers with the Franciscan Sisters in Little Falls. Donors are always welcomed and needed to help the Franciscans further their mission to serve the poor and those on the margins of society.